OVERCOMING DOUBT

DR. NEIL T. ANDERSON

Regal

From Gospel Light
Ventura, California, U.S.A.

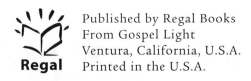

Published by Regal Books
From Gospel Light
Ventura, California, U.S.A.
Printed in the U.S.A.

Regal Books is a ministry of Gospel Light, a Christian publisher dedicated to serving the local church. We believe God's vision for Gospel Light is to provide church leaders with biblical, user-friendly materials that will help them evangelize, disciple and minister to children, youth and families.

It is our prayer that this Regal book will help you discover biblical truth for your own life and help you meet the needs of others. May God richly bless you.

For a free catalog of resources from Regal Books/Gospel Light, please call your Christian supplier or contact us at 1-800-4-GOSPEL *or* www.regalbooks.com.

Cover and interior design by Robert Williams
Edited by Amy Spence

Library of Congress Cataloging-in-Publication Data

Anderson, Neil T., 1942–
  Overcoming doubt / Neil T. Anderson.
    p. cm.
Includes bibliographical references.
  ISBN 0-8307-3254-3
  1. Faith. 2. Belief and doubt. I. Title.
  BT774.A54 2004
  234'.23—dc22   2003022834

1 2 3 4 5 6 7 8 9 10 11 12 13 14 15 / 10 09 08 07 06 05 04

Rights for publishing this book in other languages are contracted by Gospel Light Worldwide, the international nonprofit ministry of Gospel Light. Gospel Light Worldwide also provides publishing and technical assistance to international publishers dedicated to producing Sunday School and Vacation Bible School curricula and books in the languages of the world. For additional information, visit www.gospellightworldwide.org; write to Gospel Light Worldwide, P.O. Box 3875, Ventura, CA 93006; or send an e-mail to info@gospellightworldwide.org.

CONTENTS

INTRODUCTION

The phone rang shortly before noon. The congregation of the church had extended a call for me to be their senior pastor. I answered that call, leaving an exciting ministry where I had worn several hats: I started out as the college pastor, picked up the youth ministry and finally became the minister of adult education in a large multistaffed church. Now I was going to be the senior pastor in a struggling church plant that was meeting in the facilities of a Seventh-day Adventist Church.

The church was six years old. The founding pastor left after four years, leaving the flock without a shepherd for two years. They had pieced together a couple of irregularly shaped acres in a residential area in the hopes of building a church there. Nobody was too excited about the property, but land was at a premium in this coastal community of Southern California. I had my doubts about the possibility of ever building there.

Six months into the ministry, I sensed that God was going to do what could not be explained by hard work or human ingenuity. I even shared my impressions with the congregation. They surely had their doubts.

THE INFORMANT

While studying in my office for a Sunday message, my secretary informed me that a realtor wanted to see me. He represented a construction firm looking for available space to build houses. He tracked us down to see if we would be willing to sell our fragmented property, so they could build a new housing development.

Given the difficulty of finding available property, I informed him that we wouldn't be interested in selling. He asked if we especially wanted that particular property, or if we would be willing to build somewhere else. I felt a little uncomfortable speaking for the church, but I didn't like our property or its location. We chatted for a while and he left with the impression that we would be willing to sell the property if he could find something better suited for us.

A week later he wanted to show me a piece of property that he thought would be much better for us, because it was larger and in a better location. To my surprise, he showed me five vacant acres situated perfectly in the cross section of our ministry. I was hesitant to find out the asking price. He thought the price would be reasonable since it had been tied up in litigation. A bank had repossessed the property and held it for 10 years while paying the taxes. I asked him to give us a bid for our old property. It was time to inform the church board.

The board was as pleased and surprised as I was that such property was still available. The church met and we all agreed to bid for the property, but we were not to exceed $500,000. Ours was a middle- to upper-middle-class coastal community in 1978, but we all had our doubts that we could actually purchase that property for such a low price. We started negotiations with the bank by making an offer of $400,000, and we were pleasantly surprised to receive an offer of $325,000 for our old property. For $75,000, we could double our acreage and move to a much better location.

Friday morning I heard that the bank had turned down our bid. I drove to the bank to retrieve the offer and asked if the person responsible for the property was there. He was, and he invited me into his office. I felt led to say, "We are just a nickel-and-dime operation, and I am authorized to counteroffer $425,000. Are we wasting our time?" He informed me that three vice presidents, of which he was one, had to agree, and one of the other two was in the bank. He excused himself to talk with the other vice president. Less than five minutes later he came back with a signed and amended contract for $425,000. I was elated and so was the church. For $100,000, we had received what we thought unimaginable weeks earlier.

THE NEWS

While waiting for the contracts to close, we formed a building committee and started making plans for this gift from God. Days before we were supposed to close on our old property, the realtor paid me another visit with some very bad news. The contractor he represented was backing out of the deal. "Could he do that?" I asked. The realtor thought the contractor legally could and shared how sorry he was. "I have represented him for 25 years and he has never done this before. I think he is having some family problems. His daughter has multiple sclerosis and is living with them since her husband left her."

I shared the news that Sunday morning with the board; they were upset. Several members wanted to pursue legal action against the contractor. I was deeply disappointed in them, and I said I would have no part in any litigation. Our ministry was to help hurting people, not sue them! The next Tuesday I held my regular visitation evangelism class, and I could sense the Lord leading me to visit the contractor, whom I had never met. To my surprise, his phone number and address were listed in the phone book.

I drove to the address listed, doubting that I would have any chance to see him in this upscale community, since most of the homes were gated. To my surprise, his wasn't! The house was so huge that I wasn't sure where the front door was. As I walked by the kitchen window, his maid saw me and asked through the open window what I was doing there. She invited me to the front door, but I had to ask where it was! I said I was there to see the contractor. He wasn't home, but his wife and daughter were, so she invited me in. In their large master bedroom, I met his wife and daughter, who was obviously physically impaired.

I introduced myself and said to the wife, "I have never met your husband, but we had a business deal that fell through. I sensed that he was hurting, and I wanted to come by to see if I could do anything to help." I then found out that the mother and daughter were attending a cult religious group, but I noticed that they were reading Chuck Colson's book *Born Again*. An hour later, I had the privilege of leading them both to Christ.

I nearly flew off that mountain of affluence in my pastoral limousine, which was a Volkswagen Bug. The next day the realtor called and said, "I don't know what you did yesterday, but the deal is back on. But he has lowered his offer to $300,000." We gladly accepted what was still a very good deal.

A TEST

It was a test. God wanted to give us that property, but He wanted to know what we would do with it. Eight thousand people lived within a four-block radius of that location, and He wanted us to be a beacon of light for the lost.

I had lunch with another realtor who was also the third-term mayor of the city. I asked him about the possibility of getting a builder's permit for a church. He shared that our parcel was one of four plots that had been in litigation for about 10 years. A large contracting firm had wanted to build low-income housing on the property, but the city quickly rezoned to stop that from happening. Therefore, this prime property sat vacant for 10 years with neither side moving. He advised us to sell the property, because he had serious doubts about our ever obtaining the city's permission to build. His advice could have been a lethal blow to my faith, given what I perceived to be God's leading.

Around the same time, I received another caller at our church office. This man was a lawyer who represented a large construction firm. They were about to make a deal with the city to stop the litigation if the city would let them build condominiums. This construction firm owned the other three plots and wanted to buy ours, which I informed them was not for sale. They offered us $750,000, and I was beginning to wonder if I was in the wrong business!

The construction company proceeded to make plans with and presentations to the city's planning committee; and our church leaders attended, following the proceedings with great interest. Some serious zoning questions arose that affected how the residential community interfaced with commercial businesses. During one meeting, a council member pointed out that it would be a lot easier if we exchanged our five acres with one of the five-acre plots the construction company owned. Consequently, the construction firm offered to exchange five of their acres for ours, clear the proposed new property of all debris, give us fill dirt for a low spot and pay us $200,000 cash.

We agreed, especially since our architect said the new property was in a better location.

To our delight, we started our building program with the property debt free, the ground cleared and $75,000 cash in our pockets. Halfway through construction, our contractor said he had played golf the previous weekend with an old friend who asked him what he was doing. He said, "I'm building a church building" and shared with him the location. His friend said, "You are not going to believe this. The pastor of that church struck a deal for that property [the original lot] for $425,000 a couple years back, and that same afternoon I submitted a bid of $600,000 for the same property."

THE TRUTH

When you read a story like the one above, what comes to your mind? Do you doubt it? Do you believe that it actually happened—which it did—and are therefore grateful and encouraged that God is still building His Church? Do you think that kind of thing only happens to others, but not to you?

Why do we doubt God? God said He would build His Church, and even the gates of hell couldn't keep that from happening (see Matt. 16:18). He said He would meet all our needs (see Phil. 4:19). If God is truth—and He cannot lie—then why do we doubt Him?

Acquiring new property and building new facilities in my first pastorate is just one of hundreds of experiences that have confirmed to me that the Bible is true, that God loves us and that we can totally trust Him. I have witnessed God bind up the brokenhearted and set captives free right in front of my eyes. As an ex-aerospace engineer and holder of five earned degrees, I have yet to find any logical incongruities in God's Word, which is truly amazing, since God inspired His prophets to write the

Bible over a period of 1,500 years. The Dead Sea Scrolls have proved how accurate God's Word has been preserved for thousands of years. This remarkable find has given us a manuscript dating back to one year and possibly 200 years before Christ. I have visited the museum in Jerusalem and seen the entire book of Isaiah in one complete scroll, which is a stern rebuke to all the liberals who were "sure" that Isaiah was originally two or three books written by two or three different authors.

THE BIG QUESTION

Is doubting wrong? If it were, we would all be wrong, because we all have experienced some doubts. Doubting is part of our faith journey; it plays a role in every Christian's experience. In this book, I will explore the nature of doubt and how it differs from unbelief. However, this is primarily a book about faith, so I will explain the nature of faith and how we all live by faith every day. The real question is, What or whom do we believe? We will consider how our faith works on a daily basis and how we can know whether our walk of faith is in line with God's Word. I also will address the issue of doubt and mental health. Finally, I will look at the spiritual implications of doubt and expose the spiritual battle for our minds, which is intended to destroy our faith.

Perhaps an illustration will reveal the tension that we all have when it comes to faith. The story is told of Pistol Pete who ventured out on a six-day hike across a barren desert. He was told by reputable sources that there was water halfway across the trek, so he carried enough water for him and his horse to last three days. Sure enough he came to the promised well, but as he pumped the handle, it only burped up sand.

Then he noticed a sign attached to the pump that read "Two feet straight north and two feet down is a bottle of water. Dig it up and use the water to prime the pump. Then fill the bottle for the next person and bury it in the same location."

Do you trust the sign? Will you use the water to prime the pump; or will you drink the water in the bottle giving you and your horse just enough water to cross the remaining distance? Do you take God at His Word and live accordingly for eternity, with the promise of future rewards? Or do you doubt that He exists and live for the pleasures of this passing world? It's your choice.

CHAPTER ONE

THE NATURE OF DOUBT

Give me the benefit of your convictions, if you have any, but keep
your doubts to yourself, for I have enough of my own.

JOHANN WOLFGANG VON GOETHE

The Lord had just heard that His herald and friend John the Baptist had been beheaded. The news moved Jesus to seek time alone; He withdrew to a desolate place. But news traveled fast and a large crowd followed Him on foot. Overlooking His own needs, He felt compassion for them and healed many.

Evening came and His disciples were concerned that the crowd, which had swollen to 5,000, had nothing to eat. They suggested that Jesus send the crowd away. "But Jesus said to them, 'They do not need to go away; you give them something to eat!'" (Matt. 14:16). How were these men going to feed 5,000

> # WHEN CONFRONTED WITH WHAT APPEARS TO BE AN IMPOSSIBLE TASK, HOW DO WE TYPICALLY RESPOND?

people with their limited resources? When confronted with what appears to be an impossible task, how do we typically respond? If we don't believe we have the resources to do it, doubts quickly turn to unbelief. The truth is, without the presence of Christ in our lives, we won't ever have the resources to do God's will. We can perform what appear to be Christian duties in our own strength and with our own resources, but nothing we accomplish by that means will last for eternity.

It is human nature to consider only our resources when confronted with any task. In the things we can do, we have no or few doubts. The disciples assessed their resources and reported that they had only five loaves of bread and two fish (see Matt. 14:17).

"Ordering the people to sit down on the grass, He took the five loaves and the two fish, and looking up toward heaven, He blessed the food, and breaking the loaves He gave them to the disciples, and the disciples gave them to the crowds" (Matt. 14:19). The 5,000 were fed and the disciples even picked up leftovers—each man had a basketful. What an object lesson! Did they learn from it? Were all their doubts erased?

After sending the multitudes away, Jesus sent the disciples across the Sea of Galilee and then went up on the mountain to pray (see Matt. 14:23). Later in the night, the disciples rowed against a storm, getting nowhere. Jesus walked across the water to the disciples, and Mark records, "He intended to pass by them" (6:48). Jesus intends to pass by the self-sufficient. Do we want to row against the storms of life and hope to survive by our own strength and resources? We can go ahead; God will let us. We can row until our arms fall off, but eventually the storms will bring us down. Or we can call upon the name of the Lord and be saved. The disciples called upon the Lord and the water was calmed. Mark records:

> They had not gained any insight from the incident of the loaves, but their heart was hardened (6:52).

WHY DO WE DOUBT?

When the disciples first saw Jesus walking on the lake, they thought he was a ghost; they were afraid. Jesus said, "Take courage, it is I; do not be afraid" (Matt. 14:27). The impulsive Peter was so relieved and excited that he asked Jesus to command that he come to Him on the water. Jesus said, "Come" (Matt. 14:29), and Peter did. At least he did for a few steps, until He took His eyes off Jesus and felt the effects of the wind. As Peter started to sink, he cried out for Jesus to save him. The Lord stretched out His hand and said, "You of little faith, why did you doubt?" (Matt. 14:31). Why did he doubt? Why do we?

We need to put this in perspective. The twelve disciples witnessed Jesus heal the sick, feed the 5,000 and calm the sea. He demonstrated His authority over demons, diseases, death and nature, and still they doubted. When the resurrected Christ appeared to many people, many of them "worshiped him; but some doubted" (Matt. 28:17, *NIV*). Even John the Baptist struggled with doubts and sent two of his disciples to ask Jesus, "Are You the Expected One, or do we look for someone else?" (Luke 7:19). Jesus responded:

> Go and report to John what you have seen and heard: the blind receive sight, the lame walk, the lepers are cleansed, and the deaf hear, the dead are raised up, the poor have the gospel preached to them (v. 22).

Is it any wonder that people doubt today when we haven't seen or witnessed any such miracles? Jesus said to doubting Thomas, "Because you have seen Me, have you believed? Blessed are they who did not see, and yet believed" (John 20:29). What we have today is the witness of credible people who have seen, heard, touched and were transformed by the love of God. We also have the testimony of believers for 20 centuries, and the internal witness of the Holy Spirit who leads us into all truth (see John 16:13).

WHAT IS DOUBT?

Doubt can be defined as the absence of both assent (agreement) and dissent (disagreement) to a certain proposition. It is the lack of commitment to believe or not to believe. For example, Thomas had not seen the resurrected Christ when it was reported that the others disciples had seen Him. Thomas said, "Unless I see in His hands the imprint of the nails, and put my finger into the place of the nails, and put my hand into His side, I will not believe" (John 20:25). When Thomas made this statement, he was not doubting. He already had made his decision—"I will not believe." His colleagues' words were not enough to sway him. He wanted physical evidence.

Doubt is when the evidence of pro and con is evenly balanced. Such doubt is a prelude to belief or a precursor to unbelief. The journey of faith begins with doubt—such doubt is not unbelief. Unbelief is a conviction about something or someone, which is in itself a belief. To say "I don't believe in God" is a conviction that there is no God, which is a belief. Therefore, doubt does not imply unbelief. It simply means that one is unconvinced.

Jesus consistently condemned unbelief whenever and wherever He found it. Yet He tolerated doubt, because it was transitory—a nonpermanent state of mind. We must be careful, however, because the word "unbelief" in the Bible can refer to doubt. That is probably the case in Mark 9, in which the desperate father asked for help:

> "If you can do anything, take pity on us and help us!" And Jesus said to him, "If You can?" All things are possible to him who believes. Immediately the boy's father cried out and said, "I do believe; help my unbelief" (vv. 22-24).

Jesus didn't condemn the boy's father for doubting; He just assured him that all things are possible with God. The man's cry for help for his unbelief is better thought of as doubt.

Thomas became convinced when the Lord said to him, "Reach here with your finger, and see My hands; and reach here your hand and put it into My side; and do not be unbelieving, but believing" (John 20:27). The evidence overwhelmed Thomas. He moved from unbelief to belief, saying, "My Lord and my God!" (v. 28). Thomas was confronted with something more than physical evidence, since it is *doubtful* that any of the disciples told Jesus what Thomas had said. His response indicated more than a belief in Jesus' resurrection. Proclaiming Jesus as Lord (*Kurios* is the New Testament equivalent of the Old Testament "Jehovah") and God (*Theos*), Thomas declared his belief in the divinity of Jesus.

BEYOND A REASONABLE DOUBT?

Have you ever noticed that nobody lives by doubt? We live by faith in someone or something, or we don't live very well. Doubt leads to inaction; belief moves to action. This is partially what James was referring to when he wrote "I will show you my faith by my works" (2:18). What can you show for your doubts; and how much is accomplished by those of us who lack confidence in anyone or anything?

> DOUBT LEADS TO INACTION;
> BELIEF MOVES TO ACTION.

Many of us who doubt struggle with decision making, but those of us who have great faith are decisive and take action. For example, Joshua, a servant of God, was such a great leader because he never sat on the fence. When an angel, appearing in the form of a man, stood in front of Joshua with a sword drawn in his hand, "Joshua went to him and said to him, 'Are you for us or for our adversaries?'" (Josh. 5:13). The angel identified himself as the captain of the host of the Lord and commanded Joshua to remove his shoes, for Joshua stood on holy ground. Joshua did so. He believed and obeyed.

Joshua also taught his belief to others:

Now, therefore, fear the LORD and serve Him in sincerity and truth; and put away the gods which your fathers served beyond the River and in Egypt, and serve the LORD. If it is disagreeable in your sight to serve the LORD, choose for yourselves today whom you will serve: whether the gods which your fathers served which were beyond the River, or the gods of the Amorites in whose land you are living; but as for me and my house, we will serve the LORD (24:14-15).

Great leaders do not waver in unbelief. Some doubters may think they are leaders, but nobody is following them. Can any of us imagine a team on the sidelines in a close game listening to a coach who can't decide what play to run next? Where's the inspiration in that? The problem is, people will follow someone of strong conviction regardless of what they believe. If that person or cause is passionate enough, people will follow. Why do people like Hitler come to power? Hitler was decisive and filled with confidence. Germany's terrible state in the years following World War I demanded leadership—someone who could get the country back on track to world dominance. Hitler persauded his followers to believe that they were a superrace—to their detriment and that of the world.

Athletes usually believe their coaches if their coaches have proven themselves superior in their sport. Coaches don't have to be former champions themselves—they can be just as effective as leaders or more so if they have produced champions or championship teams. Athletes will do whatever their coaches say, because they believe their coaches are right. When coaches challenge techniques and suggest changes, athletes will adjust even if at first it feels awkward. We move from doubt to belief based on the track record of our leaders. When we truly believe in an authority figure, we will follow in complete obedience.

On the contrary, when doubt pervades an individual, it is called skepticism or definitive doubt. The skeptic despairs of ever knowing truth with certainty. This is the downside of post-modernism. In secular education and the media, the idea that no absolute truth exists is the prevailing philosophy—which is essentially the same as saying there is no God. This idea leads to ambivalence, which is just another form of doubt. An ambivalent society doesn't care. Ambivalent people are emotionally flat. They have no convictions and no purpose for living.

WHO ARE THE BLESSING SNATCHERS?

The reason doubt pervades society is because doubt is easier to establish than faith. The devil has the easier job. For instance, defense lawyers don't have to prove innocence. All they have to do is establish a reasonable doubt and the jury is obligated to acquit the defendant. On the other hand, to convict someone, prosecutors have to prove that the accused is guilty beyond rea-sonable doubt.

If we want to paralyze a society, then all we would have to do is create a little doubt. The message believed by the ineffective, inactive and insignificant is, When in doubt, don't do anything. Most doubting people aren't doing anything of consequence.

Doubt is fostered by the father of lies (we will look at his role in chapter 7), and he has a lot of helpers. The following are examples of how the world is filled with blessing snatchers:

I see you bought a new suit. I bought one there and a sleeve fell off.

You bought a new car from that dealer? I did and it was a lemon.

So, you've become a Christian. Now you have an enemy you never had before. I tried it once, but it didn't work.

We planned a picnic, so it will probably rain again.

A pessimistic attitude can also snatch blessings and it has been estimated that 95 percent of the world's population are pessimists by nature. Pessimism is supported by the world's system. Weatherpersons report a 30 percent chance of rain tomorrow, but they seldom if ever report a 70 percent chance of sunshine. The news anchor reports all the bad news, but he or she seldom reports any of the good deeds done daily by the faithful. The media can't resist reporting about a fallen pastor, but it almost never shares the good deeds that the vast majority of godly pastors are doing every day. This can't help but create doubts in the minds of those who are undecided.

On the contrary, optimists think they live in the best of all possible worlds—and the pessimists are afraid they are right! The pessimist asks, "What do I stand to lose if I do?" The optimist asks, "What do I stand to lose if I don't?" The pessimist sees the problem in every opportunity. The optimist sees the opportunity in every problem. Pessimists feed on doubt.

The following story illustrates this idea: Word got around heaven that the devil was holding a fire sale. Some of his best weapons were on the auction block. A couple of curious angels thought they would check out some of the items to see what the devil was up to. Of course, the primary tools of his trade—temptation, accusation and deception—were not for sale, even though they sat prominently on display for all to see. What was for sale on the pedestals included petty gossip, jealousy, arrogance, gluttony, lust and many of the devil's other well-known tricks that have defeated many of God's children. Satan's pitchmen were anxious to widely disperse them in God's kingdom for others to use.

One of the angels noticed that one pedestal was empty and asked the little devils which tool was missing. "Oh, that is discouragement," a little devil said. "We can't keep it in stock, because it is in constant use and our most effective weapon. Most of God's children already own it anyway!"

WHAT'S THE REAL DEAL WITH THE POWER OF POSITIVE THINKING?

It is a sin to take away other people's courage when they can do all things through Christ who strengthens them (see Phil. 4:13). Those who sow seeds of discouragement will reap the harvest of doubt. Dale Carnegie once said:

> If you want to change people without giving offense or arousing resentment, use encouragement. Make the fault you want to correct seem easy to correct; make the thing you want the person to do seem easy to do. . . . If you and I will inspire the people with whom we come in contact to a realization of the hidden treasure they possess, we can do far more than change people. We can literally transform them.[1]

Norman Vincent Peale is well known for having taught the power of positive thinking. Many other motivational speakers since have tied into that well-known axiom. We generally benefit from incorporating positive thinking into our lives. There is no question that what we choose to think determines what we do. We can't do anything without first thinking it: "For as he thinks within himself, so he is" (Prov. 23:7). An unknown author wrote the following poem to illustrate this principle:

If you think you are beaten—you are.
    If you think you dare not—you won't.
If you want to win but think you can't,
    It's almost a cinch you won't.
If you think you'll lose—you've lost.
    For out of the world we find,
That success begins with a fellow's will,
    It's all in the state of mind.
Life's battles don't always go,
    To the stronger or faster man,
But sooner or later the man who wins,
    Is the one who thinks he can.[2]

We as Christians have been somewhat reluctant to buy in to the power of positive thinking—and maybe for good reason. Thinking is a function of the mind and it cannot exceed its inputs and attributes. Any attempt to push the mind beyond its limitations only results in moving from the world of reality to fantasy. However, we have to be impressed with what we can do if we will only believe in ourselves. Most of us live far below our human potential. It is estimated that the average person uses only 5 percent of his or her brain capacity.

Some people (and even some pastors) in the 1950s said that humankind would never reach the moon. But when Russia launched *Sputnik*, the United States rose to the challenge. Within a few short years, not only had Americans surpassed the Russians, but also Neil Armstrong had actually set foot on the moon. The first man walking on the moon inspired a lot of confidence in what humankind could do if they only believed that they could.

About the time that the Apollo space program shut down, a new program was envisioned. I was an aerospace engineer at the time, and our company was asked to give a proposal for engineering the guidance system of the spacecraft. Originally the idea was called Shuttle Bus. The idea was to create a reentry spacecraft that could be used again and again. When the government first issued proposals and requested bids from aerospace companies, the technology to build such a craft didn't exist. However, flush with the success of the Apollo space program, companies actually believed that they could do it, given enough time and money. Today, space-shuttle launching is so commonplace that the public pays little attention to it.

There seems to be no limit to what humankind can do. Endowed by the creator with incredible mental and physical powers, we have launched satellites that make global communication commonplace. We have learned how to transplant hearts, kidneys and livers, allowing people to live longer than they ever

> IF HUMANKIND CAN ACCOMPLISH MUCH WITH FAITH IN THEMSELVES, HOW MUCH MORE CAN WE ACCOMPLISH WITH FAITH IN GOD?

have. We have climbed the highest peaks, descended to the lowest depths of the ocean and probed outer space, going where no man has ever gone before. People continue to chop inches and seconds off world records that were deemed impossible decades ago. Yet, there is a limit to what finite humankind can do. We still haven't solved the problems of poverty, war, crime and corruption. Faith in science as the hope for humankind has diminished in this postmodern era.

You and I live in the "new age." Out with humanism and in with spiritism. Of course, as finite creatures we are limited, but what if we were really gods and we just needed to know it? There would be no limit to what we could do. We wouldn't need a savior; we would only need enlightenment. We could create reality with our own minds. If we believed hard enough, it would become true. *This kind of thinking is nothing more than old-fashioned occultism dressed up in New Age clothing.*

WHY IS THE POWER OF TRUTH BELIEVING A SURE THING?

Doubt can be somewhat overcome by the power of positive thinking, but positive thinking does have limits and is little more than humanism. Christians have something far greater. If humankind can accomplish much with faith in themselves, how much more can we accomplish with faith in God? We have the power of God within us to believe and to do all that God has created for us to be and to do. The power of believing truth will set us free according to Jesus. Knowing the truth and living accordingly by faith also will overcome our doubts (see John 8:32).

Someone once said that success comes in *cans* and failures in *cannots*. The following 20 *Cans* of Success, if believed and lived, will help us overcome a lot of doubts.

Twenty Cans of Success

1. Why should I say I can't when the Bible says I can do all things through Christ who gives me strength (see Phil. 4:13)?
2. Why should I worry about my needs when I know that God will take care of all my needs according to His riches in glory in Christ Jesus (see Phil. 4:19)?

3. Why should I fear when the Bible says God has not given me a spirit of fear, but of power, love and a sound mind (see 2 Tim. 1:7)?

4. Why should I lack faith to live for Christ when God has given me a measure of faith (see Rom. 12:3)?

5. Why should I be weak when the Bible says that the Lord is the strength of my life, and that I will display strength and take action because I know God (see Ps. 27:1; Dan. 11:32)?

6. Why should I allow Satan control over my life when God who is in me is far greater than he that is in the world (see 1 John 4:4)?

7. Why should I accept defeat when the Bible says that God always leads me in victory (see 2 Cor. 2:14)?

8. Why should I lack wisdom when I know that Christ became wisdom for me from God; and God gives wisdom to me generously when I ask Him for it (see 1 Cor. 1:30; Jas. 1:5)?

9. Why should I be depressed when I can have hope by remembering God's loving-kindness, compassion and faithfulness (see Lam. 3:21-23)?

10. Why should I worry and be upset when I can cast all my anxieties on Christ who cares for me (see 1 Pet. 5:7)?

11. Why should I ever be in bondage, knowing that there is freedom where the Spirit of the Lord is (see Gal. 5:1)?

12. Why should I feel condemned when the Bible says there is no condemnation for those who are in Christ Jesus (see Rom. 8:1)?

13. Why should I feel alone when Jesus said He is with me always and He will never leave me nor forsake me (see Matt. 28:20; Heb. 13:5)?

14. Why should I feel like I'm cursed or have bad luck when the Bible says that Christ rescued me from the curse of the Law that I might receive His Spirit by faith (see Gal. 3:13-14)?

15. Why should I be unhappy when I, like Paul, can learn to be content whatever the circumstances (see Phil. 4:11)?

16. Why should I feel worthless when Christ became sin for me so that I might become the righteousness of God (see 2 Cor. 5:21)?

17. Why should I feel helpless in the presence of others when I know that if God is for me, who can be against me (see Rom. 8:31)?

18. Why should I be confused when God is the author of peace and He gives me knowledge through His spirit who lives in me (see 1 Cor. 2:12; 14:33)?

19. Why should I feel like a failure when I am more than a conqueror through Christ who loves me (see Rom. 8:37)?

20. Why should I let the pressures of life bother me when I can take courage knowing that Jesus has overcome the world and its problems (see John 16:33)?[3]

GOING DEEPER

"The journey of faith begins with doubt"

1. Have you ever struggled with doubt? Explain.

2. Is doubt bad? Why or why not? *No-only if you stop action.*

3. What is the difference between doubt and unbelief? *doubt is not permanent"*

4. What does reasonable doubt lead to? Why?

5. What is the connection between doubt and indecision? *Doubt, your not convinced*

6. What are skepticism and ambivalence?
Doubt takes over   Emotionally flat "Don't Care"

doubt-your not convinced - if - you imbrief your make your choice.

7. Do you have any blessing snatchers in your life? Are you a blessing snatcher? *Sure do.*

8. Are you an optimist or a pessimist? Explain.

9. What are the benefits and potential pitfalls concerning the power of positive thinking? *Limited in our mind. need to rely on God — not our own understand.*

10. How does the power of believing truth differ from the power of positive thinking?

Truth, being God's word doesn't change. power of positive thinking is limited.

Believing in christ and knowing his truth and taking action.

"they will show their faith by their fruit."

CHAPTER TWO

THE NATURE
OF FAITH

*Faith in order, which is the basis of science, cannot be reasonably
separated from faith in the Ordainer.*

DR. ASA GRAY, AMERICAN BOTANIST

Monday, January 6

Bought a really good book about faith. It's called,
*Goodness Gracious—in God's Name, What on Earth Are We
Doing for Heaven's Sake?* A very witty title I feel.

It's all about how Christians should be able to move
mountains by faith, if they are really tuned to God. Very
inspiring.

Waited 'till there was no one around; then prac-
ticed with a paper clip. Put it on my desk and stared at
it, willing it to move. Nothing! Tried commanding it in
a loud voice.

Tuesday, January 7
Had another go with the paper clip tonight. Really
took authority over it. Couldn't get it to budge.

Told God I'd give up anything He wanted, if He
would just make it move half an inch. Nothing!

All rather worrying really. If you only need faith the
size of a mustard seed to move a mountain, what hope is
there for me when I can't even get a paper clip to do what
it's told!

Saturday, January 11
Got up early today to have a last go at that blasted
paper clip. Ended up hissing viciously at it, trying not to
wake everybody up. When I gave up and opened the
door, I found Anne and Gerald listening outside in their
night-clothes, looking quite anxious.

Anne said, "Darling, why did you tell that paper clip
you'd straighten it out if it didn't soon get its act together?"[1]

Faith is a mystery to many of us. *How do we make it work?* We
wonder. A little boy came home from church and his mother
asked him what he learned in Sunday School. He said, "My
teacher told us about Moses, who was being chased by the
Egyptians. When he came to this big sea, he built a pontoon
bridge and hurried all his people across. And when the Egyptians
came, he blew up the bridge and they all drowned." "Is that what
your teacher taught you?" asked the surprised mother. "No, but

you wouldn't believe what my teacher taught me." The little boy thought faith was believing in something untrue.

THE ESSENCE OF FAITH

In the New Testament, the English words "faith," "believe" and "trust" are all the same word—*pistis*—in the original Greek, which means believing is something more than giving mental assent or intellectual acknowledgment. Faith is a demonstrated reliance on somebody or something. Consider how important the concept of faith is to the Christian. The writer of Hebrews wrote "And without faith it is impossible to please Him, for he who comes to God must believe that He is and that He is a rewarder of those who seek Him" (11:6). Couple that with the facts that we are saved by faith (see Eph. 2:8-9) and that we "walk by faith, not by sight" (2 Cor. 5:7). In other words, faith is the basis for our salvation and the means by which we live. If we are going to live a free and victorious life in Christ, there are three operating principles of faith that we need to keep in mind.

Principle 1: Faith Depends on Its Object

Every one of us lives by faith. The only difference between Christian faith and non-Christian faith is the object of that faith. Since all of us believe something, the critical issue is *what* we believe or *who* we believe in. Telling another person to live by faith is invalid if that person has no understanding of the object of his or her faith. We can't have faith in faith. Faith is dependent on its object. How trustworthy that object has been.

The truth is, we all live every moment of every day by faith. The problem is, some of our faith objects are valid while others are not. For instance, suppose you were driving a car and see a green light. You would probably drive through the intersection without giving your choice a second thought—and you would do it by faith. First, you believed the light was red for the cars traveling in the opposite direction, even though you couldn't see it. Second, you believed the drivers coming from the opposite

> # THE ONLY DIFFERENCE BETWEEN CHRISTIAN FAITH AND NON-CHRISTIAN FAITH IS THE OBJECT OF THAT FAITH.

direction would stop at the red light. That is a lot of faith to place in a mechanical device and in humankind. If you didn't believe that the stoplight would work properly, you probably wouldn't drive through many intersections, or you would proceed very cautiously. We usually trust people or things which have proven to be reliable over a long period of time.

What happens when the object of our faith proves unreliable? We give up on it. Maybe not immediately, but how many failures would we tolerate before saying, "Never again!" Once faith is lost, it is difficult to regain. Our failure to believe isn't the problem; it's the object of our faith that has proven to be untrustworthy. It is why our relationships are so fragile. One act of unfaithfulness can all but destroy a marriage. We can forgive our spouse and commit to making the marriage work, but it will take months and even years to gain back the lost trust. We would be foolish to trust someone or something that has proven to be unreliable.

We generally have an unquestioned faith in order. The faith object most accepted by humankind is the fixed order of the universe—primarily the solar system. That is why many primitive cultures worshiped the sun, and why the Egyptians built pyramids as a pagan testimony to the sun god, Ra. Citizens of the modern world set their watches, plan their calendars and schedule their days believing that Earth will continue to revolve on its axis and rotate around the sun at its current rate. If Earth's orbit shifted just a few degrees and delayed sunrise, the whole world would be thrown into chaos. The natural laws governing the physical universe, which God created, are among our most trustworthy faith objects.

The ultimate faith object, of course, is not the sun, but the Son of God. In Hebrews 13:7 we read: "Remember those who led you, who spoke the word of God to you; and considering the result of their conduct, imitate their faith." The writer of Hebrews didn't say, "imitate what they do," because what they did is just the product of what they chose to believe. The next verse reveals what they believed: "Jesus Christ is the same yesterday and today and forever" (v. 8). The fact that God is immutable is what makes Him eminently trustworthy (see Num. 23:19; Mal. 3:6). God cannot change, nor can His Word change:

> The grass withers, the flower fades, but the word of our God stands forever (Isa. 40:8).

This eternal consistency is why God is faithful and why we put our trust in Him.

A young man who was struggling in his faith asked to schedule an appointment to speak with me. After hearing his story, I knew why he struggled. He had made a decision for Christ and a well-meaning pastor had challenged him to go and live by faith. He said, "I've been living by faith for the last three years, and it has been one continuous struggle." What is wrong with challenging people to live by faith? Faith in what? We can't have faith in faith. Faith has no validity without an object.

The same principle holds true for meditation. What is more important: meditation or the object of our meditation? It is the object, of course. The psalmist wrote, "But his delight is in the law of the LORD, and in His law he meditates day and night" (1:2). We can meditate on our navels all night and end up in la-la land. The faith object matters!

Principle 2: How Much Faith We Have Depends on How Well We Know the Object of Our Faith

When some of us struggle with faith in God, it's not because our faith object has failed or is insufficient. It is because we don't have a true knowledge of God and His ways. We expect Him to respond or answer prayer in a certain way—our way, not

> IF WE WANT OUR FAITH IN GOD TO INCREASE, WE MUST INCREASE OUR KNOWLEDGE OF GOD AND HIS WAYS.

His—and when He doesn't comply, we say, "Forget You, God." The problem is not with God. He's the perfect faith object. Faith in God fails when we hold a faulty understanding of Him and His ways.

If we want our faith in God to increase, we must increase our knowledge of God and His ways. If we have little knowledge of God and His Word, we will have little faith. If we have great knowledge of God and His Word, we potentially will have great faith. The hall of fame in Hebrews 11 depicts people who possessed great faith in God, because (1) they knew they had a great

God; and (2) they knew and believed His Word.

That is why faith cannot be pumped up. It will do you no good to admonish yourself by saying, "If only I can believe! If only I can believe!" You can believe, because belief is a choice that we all make every day. Any attempt to step out in faith beyond that which you know to be true about God and His ways is presumptuous. You choose to believe God and live according to what He says is true. The only way to increase your faith is to increase your knowledge of God, who is the only legitimate and authoritative faith object, and His Word. That is why Paul wrote: "Faith comes from hearing, and hearing by the word of Christ" (Rom. 10:17). If you know 7 promises from the Word of God, the best you can have is a 7-promise faith. If you know 7,000 promises from God's Word, you potentially can have a 7,000-promise faith. Dwight L. Moody wrote:

> I prayed for faith and thought that some day faith would come down and strike me like lightning. But faith did not seem to come. One day I read in the tenth chapter of Romans, "Faith cometh by hearing, and hearing by the Word of God." I had [up to this time] closed my Bible and prayed for faith. I now opened my Bible and began to study, and faith has been growing every since.[2]

The only limit to our faith is our knowledge and understanding of God and His ways, which grow every time we read the Bible, memorize Scripture, participate in a Bible study or meditate on His Word. Can you see the practical, tangible potential for your faith to grow as you endeavor to know God and His Word? Christian faith is only bound by the infinite nature of God! No Christian has fully comprehended God and His Word, and nobody has lived up to his or her fullest potential based on what he or she already knows to be true.

It is important to know that God is under no obligation to humankind. We can't maneuver or manipulate God through prayer. He is under obligation to Himself. He promised to remain faithful to His Covenant and His Word. We have a covenant relationship with God that we can count on being true whether we believe it or not; He will always keep His word. If God declares something to be true, we simply believe Him and live by faith according to what is true. If God doesn't say it, no amount of faith will make it so. The choice to believe God doesn't make God's Word true; instead, His Word is true, and therefore, we believe it.

Principle 3: Faith Is an Action Word

To illustrate how faith grows, consider the father who stands his young son on a table and encourages him to jump from the table into his arms. The boy may waver in unbelief for a moment but then leap into his father's arms. Then the father stands back a little bit further and asks his son to jump again—this time the step of faith is a little bit bigger. Finally, the father takes his son outside and puts him on the limb of a tree and encourages him to jump. This is an even greater leap of faith, but still the son jumps. As the child continues to climb the tree of life, can his human father be the perfect faith object? No! There is a time when most children think their parents can answer any question and defeat any foe, but they will learn that is not true.

We have an obligation as parents to do more than lead our children to a saving knowledge of our Lord Jesus Christ. We need to help them understand their spiritual identity and heritage. Their faith object changes when they become children of God. We can't always be with our children, but their heavenly Father can and is.

When the father encouraged his son to take a step of faith, did the boy believe his father would catch him? Yes. We know he believed, because he jumped. Suppose he wouldn't jump.

Suppose the father asked the son, "Do you believe I will catch you?" If the son answered yes but never jumped, did he really believe that his father would catch him? Not according to James. Such professions of faith are just wishful thinking:

> Faith, if it has no works, is dead, being by itself. But someone may well say, "You have faith and I have works; show me your faith without the works, and I will show you my faith by my works" (2:17-18).

In other words, if we really believe in God and His Word, it will affect our walk and talk. If we believe God and His Word, we will live accordingly. Everything we do is essentially a product of what we choose to believe. Some of us don't always live according to what we profess, but we do live according to what we actually believe.

DISTORTIONS OF FAITH

Faith without action is one distortion. New Age and Eastern philosophies offer another distortion of what it means to believe. New Age practitioners say, "If you believe hard enough, it will become true." Christianity says, "It is true; therefore, I believe it." Believing something doesn't make it true, and not believing something doesn't make it false. Not believing in hell, for instance, doesn't lower the temperature down there one degree.

Consider the words of Jesus in Matthew 17:20 (*NIV*):

> I tell you the truth, if you have faith as small as a mustard seed, you can say to this mountain, "Move from here to there" and it will move. Nothing will be impossible for you.

It is correct to point out that the mountain doesn't move until we say, "Move." In other words, faith doesn't work until it is acted upon, which is the point of this passage. Yet it is incorrect to assume that we can believe whatever we want and objects will move simply because we tell them to move. Such reasoning is in league with New Age philosophers, who teach that we can create reality with our minds. To do that we would have to be gods, which is exactly what they teach.

There is only one creator—only One who can speak something out of nothing into existence. With God all things are possible, and we can do all things that are consistent with His will and His Word through Christ who strengthens us (see Phil. 4:13). However, we have never been given the privilege to determine for ourselves what is true and what is God's will. In the illustration at the beginning of this chapter, our friend decided to move the paper clip by using his mind. Telekinesis is an occult

> PRAYER IS INTENDED TO BE
> A FIRST-DOWN HUDDLE
> WHERE WE SEEK GOD'S
> DIRECTION FOR OUR LIVES.

practice that tries to move matter by mental energy. Now if God told us to pray that a mountain (or any obstacle) be removed and we prayed by faith in God, the mountain would be removed because God moved it. He would have done so because it was His will, not because we alone willed it to move.

Prayer is not a fourth-down punting situation where we desperately ask God to bail us out one more time. Prayer is intended to be a first-down huddle where we seek God's direction for our lives. The prayers that God the Holy Spirit prompts us to pray are prayers that God the Father is going to answer—always.[3]

Distortions often arise when the Church is not living up to its potential. In such times, people think the Church is an infirmary. They limp along in unbelief hoping the Lord will come soon and take them out of their miserable existence. The Church is not an infirmary; it is a military outpost under orders to storm the fortresses of unbelief. Every believer is on active duty, called to take part in fulfilling the Great Commission (see Matt. 28:19-20). Thankfully, the Church has an infirmary that ministers to the weak and the wounded. But the infirmary exists for the purpose of the military outpost. Our real calling is to be change agents in the world, who take a stand, live by faith according to what God says is true and fulfill our purpose for being here.

Hudson Taylor is often credited for intoducing the gospel to China. The following is his spiritual secret to victorious Christian living in his own words:

> I felt the ingratitude, the danger, the sin of not living nearer to God. I prayed, agonized, fasted, strove, made resolutions, read the Word more diligently, sought more time for meditation—but without avail. Every day, almost every hour, the consciousness of sin oppressed me.
>
> I knew that if only I could abide in Christ all would be well, but I could not. . . . Each day brought its register of sin and failure, of lack of power. To will was indeed present within me, but how to perform I found not. . . . Then came the question, Is there no rescue? Must it be thus to the end—constant conflict, and too often defeat? . . . I hated myself, my sin, yet gained no strength against it. . . . I felt I was a child of God. . . . But to rise to my privileges as a child, I was utterly powerless.

All the time I felt assured that there was in Christ all I needed, but the practical question was—how to get it out. . . . I strove for faith, but it would not come: I tried to exercise it, but in vain. . . . I prayed for faith, but it came not. What was I to do?

When my agony of soul was at its height, a sentence in a letter from dear McCarthy was used to remove the scales from my eyes, and the Spirit of God revealed to me the truth of our oneness with Jesus as I had never known it before. (I quote from memory): "But how to get faith strengthened? Not by striving after faith, but by resting on the faithful One."

As I read, I saw it all! "If we believe not, He abideth faithful." I looked to Jesus and saw (and when I saw, oh, how the joy flowed!) that He had said, "I will never leave thee." I thought, *I have striven in vain to rest in Him. I'll strive no more.*

I am no better than before. In a sense I do not wish to be. But I am dead, buried with Christ—aye, and risen too! And now Christ lives in me and "The life that I now live in the flesh, I live by faith in the Son of God, who loved me and gave himself up for me." . . . Do not let us consider Him as far off, when God has made us one with Him, members of His Body. Nor should we look upon this experience, these truths, as for a few. They are the birthright of every child of God . . . the only power for deliverance from sin or for true service.[4]

GOING DEEPER

1. Has there ever been a testing time when you took God at His word? What happened?

2. Do you agree that everyone lives by faith? Hov faith do you think it takes to believe that the universe came about by chance?

3. Do you agree that it's who or what you put your faith in that determines whether your faith is effective? Or does the effectiveness of your faith have more to do with how much faith you have?

4. Do you think faith is a choice? Why or why not?

5. Can you think of a time when you asked God to do something, but you were disappointed because He didn't do what you had asked or didn't do it in the way you had asked? For instance, did you perhaps faithfully pray for someone to get better, but he or she died? What have you concluded from such difficult experiences?

6. Elijah said, "How long will you waver between two opinions? If the LORD is God, follow him; but if Baal is God, follow him" (1 Kings 18:21, NIV). What is keeping you from making a commitment to base your life completely on what God says is true, regardless of your feelings and the opinions of others?

FEAR OF THE
UNKNOWN

CHAPTER THREE

REASONABLE FAITH

My most cherished possession I wish I could leave you is my faith in Jesus Christ, for with Him and nothing else you can be happy, but without Him and with all else you'll never be happy.

PATRICK HENRY

We can live 40 days without food, 7 days without water and 7 minutes without air; but we can't really live a moment without hope. Dr. Victor Frankl, an Austrian psychiatrist, observed that a prisoner did not live very long after hope was lost. "But even the slightest ray of hope—the rumor of better food, a whisper about an escape—helped some of the inmates to continue living even under systematic horror."[1]

Life with Christ is an endless hope, but life without Christ is a hopeless end. The psalmist wrote, "Why are you in despair, O my soul? And why have you become disturbed within me? Hope in God, for I shall again praise Him for the help of His presence" (42:5). Hope is not wishful thinking; it is the present assurance of some future good. Hebrews 6:17-19 (*NIV*) reads:

> Because God wanted to make the unchanging nature of his purpose very clear to the heirs of what was promised, he confirmed it with an oath. God did this so that, by two unchangeable things in which it is impossible for God to lie, we who have fled to take hold of the hope offered to us may be greatly encouraged. We have this hope as an anchor for the soul, firm and secure.

The two unchangeable things are God's promise and the oath confirming His promise. Our hope in God is the anchor for our souls; it moves us from doubt to belief. If God cannot lie, then the basis for our hope is found in the truth of His nature, character and Word. God cannot change, but our perceptions or understanding of Him can, which is the basis for doubt.

David wrote in Psalm 13:1: "How long, O LORD? Will You forget me forever?" David doubts God's love and concern for him in the midst of his trials. The doubt is fed by a faulty understanding of God. How can an omniscient and omnipresent God forget him for a moment much less forever? Yet David overcomes his doubt, because he chooses to believe based on God's faithfulness in the past: "But I have trusted in Your lovingkindness; my heart shall rejoice in Your salvation. I will sing to the LORD, because He has dealt bountifully with me" (vv. 5-6). Notice that David is decisive—"I will"—and confident for the future. His faith is built on God's true attributes. He sees through the eyes of faith that all is going to be well in the future.

Hope is the parent of faith. We do not step out in faith if we have no hope. Suppose you want to catch a bus that is scheduled to come by a local bus stop at 11:00 A.M. By faith you leave your apartment at 10:45 A.M., hoping to catch the bus. If the bus doesn't show and you find out that the schedule is wrong, your

> HOPE IS THE PARENT OF FAITH. WE DO NOT STEP OUT IN FAITH IF WE HAVE NO HOPE.

hope will be dashed. If it happens more than once, you probably will lose your faith in the public transportation system. Essentially, if you had no hope of catching the bus, you would not have proceeded by faith. Martin Luther wrote:

> Everything that is done in the world is done in hope. No husbandman would sow one grain of corn if he hoped not it would grow up and become seed; no bachelor would marry a wife if he hoped not to have children; no merchant or tradesman would set himself to work if he did not hope to reap benefit thereby.[2]

The biblical connection with hope is found in Hebrews 11:1: "Now faith is the assurance of things hoped for, the conviction of things not seen." In order to explain, return to the traffic-light illustration from chapter 2. When you come to an intersection, don't you hope the opposite direction has a red light, even though you can't see it? Don't you hope the cross traffic will see the light and stop? Based on that hope, you drive through the intersection by faith. If you didn't have that hope, would you proceed by faith? Driving through the intersection demonstrates your faith in an electromechanical device and in other people, which is a lot of faith since neither are totally reliable.

Hebrews 11:1 also brings out two critical issues: assurance and conviction. First, I will focus on the assurance of salvation, which is the primary doubt that keeps us from progressing in our faith. Second, we will examine the issue of conviction—are you convinced of what you believe and what it would take for you to be convinced? Let's discuss these two concepts for the remainder of the chapter.

ASSURANCE

Salvation is a definitive experience. When we receive Jesus into our lives (see John 1:12), we are born again (see John 3:3). At that very moment, we are rescued from the dominion of darkness, brought into the kingdom of God, redeemed and forgiven of our sins (see Col. 1:13-14). We are no longer "in Adam" (1 Cor. 15:22, *NIV*). We are new creations "in Christ" (2 Cor. 5:17, *NIV*), and our names are recorded in the "Lamb's book of life" (Rev. 21:27).

> And this is the testimony: God has given us eternal life, and this life is in his Son. He who has the Son has life; he who does not have the Son of God does not have life (1 John 5:11-12, *NIV*).

God wants us, His children, to be assured of our salvation: "I write these things to you who believe in the name of the Son of God so that you may know that you have eternal life" (1 John 5:13, *NIV*). Essentially, there are three means by which we are assured of our salvation: (1) the witness of Scripture, (2) the witness of the Spirit, and (3) the witness of a changed life.

The Witness of Scripture

God took the initiative to provide for our salvation; He established the criteria by which we can experience it; and He revealed the plan for both in His authoritative Word.

God secured our salvation by sacrificing His only Son to die in our place for our sins. Then, by His power, God resurrected Christ in order that we may have eternal life in Him. We can experience salvation by believing in the finished work of Christ: "Everyone who believes that Jesus is the Christ is born of God" (1 John 5:1, *NIV*). We are not saved by how we behave; we are saved by what we believe. Saving faith, however, is not just giving mental assent to what we choose to believe; saving faith is relying on the death and resurrection of Christ as the only means for salvation.

The apostle Paul wrote:

> If you confess with your mouth, "Jesus is Lord," and believe in your heart that God raised him from the dead, you will be saved. For it is with your heart that you believe and are justified, and it is with your mouth that you confess and are saved (Rom. 10:9-10, *NIV*).

We can mentally acknowledge that a historical person named Jesus died for our sins and rose again—and not be born again. Believing that Jesus is Lord is not the same as believing that Jesus is "my Lord." Jesus is the Savior, but those of us who are saved confess Jesus as the Lord of our lives and live accordingly by faith. What we choose to believe affects our walk and our talk. If it doesn't, we really don't believe.

John teaches that born-again men and women love the Father and the Son (see 1 John 5:1), and those who love the Father "obey his commands. And his commands are not burdensome, for everyone born of God overcomes the world" (1 John: 3-4, *NIV*).

"Who is it that overcomes the world? Only he who believes that Jesus is the Son of God" (v. 5).

The Witness of the Spirit

"It is the Spirit who bears witness, because the Spirit is truth" (1 John 5:6, *NKJV*). God made it possible for us to have a relationship with Him. He wants us to be assured that we are His children, if indeed we are born again. We may think we are saved, and others may acknowledge that belief, but only God has the authority to confirm our status before Him—and He does. For if we are true believers, "The Spirit Himself testifies with our spirit that we are children of God" (Rom. 8:16). Our human spirit is in union with God when we are born again, providing a subjective confirmation that we are indeed children of God:

> Because you are sons, God sent the Spirit of his Son into our hearts, the Spirit who calls out, "Abba, Father" (Gal. 4:6, *NIV*).

This inner witness is far more than a subjective feeling. The presence of the Holy Spirit in our lives brings a new love for God and a progressive detachment from the sinful attractions of this world: "For everyone born of God overcomes the world" (1 John 5:4, *NIV*). Those of us who are true believers cannot continue in sin without being convicted by the Holy Spirit. When we struggle to overcome sin's entrapment we often question our salvation, but the very fact that our sinful behavior bothers us may be the best evidence that we are born again. The Holy Spirit cannot take up residence in our lives and silently sit by while we continue to defile the temple of God. If we as Christians continue to live in sin, we are miserable; we hate the sin that holds us in bondage. "The world and its desires pass away, but the man who does the will of God lives forever" (1 John 2:17, *NIV*).

Becoming a new Christian is like getting married. We fall in love with our spouse and nothing else matters. We do things to please the other person. This newly established relationship is the most important thing in our lives—everything else revolves

> OUR SERVICE *FOR* GOD CAN ACTUALLY BECOME THE GREATEST HINDRANCE OF OUR DEVOTION *TO* GOD.

around it. But any relationship can easily degenerate into ritualistic routines of life. Doing church work and observing religious rituals are not the same as loving God. Our service *for* God can actually become the greatest hindrance of our devotion *to* God. The apostle John rebukes the Church in Ephesus for having lost their first love. He calls them to repent and do again the deeds they did when they were new believers. John concludes by saying:

> He who has an ear, let him hear what the Spirit says to the churches. To him who overcomes, I will give the right to eat from the tree of life, which is in the paradise of God (Rev. 2:7, *NIV*).

The presence of the Holy Spirit in our lives as believers is what defines the Church: "Those who are led by the Spirit of God are sons of God" (Rom. 8:14, *NIV*).

The Holy Spirit's presence also brings born-again believers a new desire to read God's Word, along with the ability to understand it:

wow!

The man without the Spirit does not accept the things that come from the Spirit of God, for they are foolishness to him, and he cannot understand them, because they are spiritually discerned (1 Cor. 2:14, *NIV*).

The Holy Spirit is the Spirit of truth (see John 14:17), and "He will guide you into all the truth" (16:13). This truth will confirm your status with your heavenly Father and set you free (see 8:32).

The Witness of a Changed Life

Salvation brings a definitive change at the very core of our being. We are new creations in Christ, which becomes evident in the way we think, feel and behave. Our desires change and we begin to clean up our language. Others begin to sense a difference in our demeanor as well as our behavior. John says, "Anyone who does what is good is from God. Anyone who does what is evil has not seen God" (3 John 1:11, *NIV*). James writes, "What good is it, my brothers, if a man claims to have faith but has no deeds?" (2:14, *NIV*). We are saved by faith, but "faith by itself, if it is not accompanied by action, is dead. . . . Show me your faith without deeds, and I will show you my faith by what I do" (vv. 17-18, *NIV*). James is not challenging the doctrine of justification by faith. He is simply saying that if we truly believe God and trust Him for our salvation, it will affect our walk and our talk.

It is important to understand the difference between having a relationship with God and living in harmony with Him. When we were physically born, we became children of our natural fathers through no choice of our own. Is there anything we could do to change that biological fact? What if we ran away from home or disavowed that they were ever our fathers? The fact that we are blood related to our fathers cannot be altered by what we say or do. However, what we say or do does affect whether or not we live in harmony with our biological fathers. If we trust and obey our fathers, we will live in harmony with them. But even if we don't, they are still our fathers, although a life of disobedience will not be a very pleasant experience for us.

The same holds true in our relationship with God. We are spiritually related to God through the blood of our Lord Jesus Christ (see 1 Pet. 1:18-19). "For you have been born again, not of perishable seed, but of imperishable, through the living and enduring word of God" (v. 23, *NIV*). Our new birth means that we are "children born not of natural descent, nor of human decision or a husband's will, but born of God" (John 1:13, *NIV*). "For we are God's workmanship, created in Christ Jesus to do good works, which God prepared in advance for us to do" (Eph. 2:10, *NIV*). He chose us, adopted us into His family and made us children of God:

> Having believed, you were marked in him with a seal, the promised Holy Spirit, who is a deposit guaranteeing our inheritance until the redemption of those who are God's possession—to the praise of his glory (Eph. 1:13-14, *NIV*).

As children of God, is there anything we can do that will affect the harmony of our relationship with our heavenly Father? Yes. And just like our relationship with our earthly father, harmony is a separate issue from relatedness. We will live in harmony with our heavenly Father if we trust and obey Him. If we fail to perfectly trust or obey Him, we will not lose our salvation, but we will lose our daily victory and rob ourselves of His blessings.

THE SINNER'S PRAYER

Salvation is a gift from God. It is free because Jesus paid the price. He did for us what we could not do for ourselves:

> For it is by grace you have been saved, through faith—
> and this not from yourselves, it is the gift of God—not by
> works, so that no one can boast (Eph. 2:8-9, *NIV*).

Grace is God's unmerited, free and spontaneous love for the spiritually dead and sinful inhabitants of this fallen world— revealed and made effective through Jesus Christ. We can't earn grace; we can only humbly receive it as a free gift.

In our sinful state, we can only throw ourselves on the mercy of God. If by the grace of God we receive mercy in this lifetime, we shall not have to face what we justly deserve in eternity. If God gave us what we deserve, we would all reap eternal damnation. The good news:

> He saved us, not because of righteous things we had
> done, but because of his mercy (Titus 3:5, *NIV*).

> Everyone who calls on the name of the Lord will be saved
> (Rom. 10:13, *NIV*).

> Yet to all who received him, to those who believed in his
> name, he gave the right to become children of God (John
> 1:12, *NIV*).

You can receive Christ right now—if you haven't already—by choosing to believe that Jesus died on the cross for your sins and was resurrected in order that you may have eternal life. You can express your choice to trust only in Christ and receive Him into your life by saying the following prayer:

> *Dear heavenly Father, I confess that I have sinned and that I*
> *am a sinner by nature. I know that I am spiritually dead*
> *because of my sin and not worthy to be Your child. I am in*

great need of Your grace and I throw myself on Your mercy.
I am sorry for my sins, and I humbly ask for Your forgiveness.
I choose to believe that Jesus died on the cross for my sins; and
I choose to believe that He came to give me eternal life. As an
act of faith, I receive You into my life and I pray that You
would enable me to be the person that You created me to be.
I choose from this day forward to repent by turning away from
sin and to live a righteous life by faith in the power of the Holy
Spirit. I ask all this in the wonderful name of Jesus, whom
I confess to be my Lord and my Savior. Amen.

Did you call on the name of the Lord? Do you believe in your heart that Jesus died for your sins and that He was raised from the dead in order that you may have eternal life? Is Jesus the Lord of your life? If you can say yes to these questions, then you are a

> ONE PERSON WITH DEEP
> CONVICTIONS IS WORTH MORE
> THAN A HUNDRED PEOPLE
> WITH ONLY A PREFERENCE
> AND A THOUSAND PEOPLE
> WITH ONLY AN INTEREST.

child of God and a member of the Body of Christ. Welcome to the family of God. There is nothing more to do to ensure your salvation, because you have not been saved by your good deeds. Salvation is a free gift from God and you have just received it. All God asks of you is to be the person He created you to be and to glorify Him by living a righteous life. Why don't you thank Him for sending Jesus to die in your place in order that you may be forgiven and have eternal life?

CONVICTION

One person with deep convictions is worth more than a hundred people with only a preference and a thousand people with only an interest. Convictions are the driving force for action. What we live are our convictions.

Consider Paul, who suffered greatly as an apostle. While he was in a Roman prison for his convictions, he wrote in 2 Timothy 1:12:

> For this reason I also suffer these things, but I am not ashamed; for I know whom I have believed and I am convinced that He is able to guard what I have entrusted to Him until that day.

Even in the most dismal of circumstances, Paul was convinced of what he believed. Later in the epistle, he admonishes Timothy:

> You, however, continue in the things you have learned and become convinced of, knowing from whom you have learned them, and that from childhood you have known the sacred writings which are able to give you the wisdom that leads to salvation through faith which is in Christ Jesus (3:14-15).

What would it take to convince you? Would the fulfillment of prophecy do it? God's Word says: "I declared the former things long ago and they went forth from My mouth, and I proclaimed them. Suddenly I acted, and they came to pass" (Isa. 48:3). God spoke in the Old Testament and then suddenly acted out His proclamations in the life of Christ. Psalm 41:9 declares Jesus would be betrayed by a friend. Zechariah 11:12-13 says Jesus would be sold for 30 pieces of silver and that the money would be thrown to the potter in the Lord's house—"that magnificent price at which" God's life was valued. Zechariah 13:7 records that Jesus would be forsaken by His disciples. True to His word, God's prophecies all came to pass. Consider all of the fulfilled prophecies in only one chapter of John's Gospel, as shown in the following table:

Event in the Life of Christ	Prophecy	Fulfillment
Mocked	see Psalm 22:7-8	see John 19:1-3
Silent before His accusers	see Isaiah 53:7	see John 19:9
Fell weak under the Cross	see Psalm 109:24-25	see John 19:17
Crucified with thieves	see Isaiah 53:9,12	see John 19:18
Garments parted and lots cast	see Psalm 22:18	see John 19:23-24
Suffered from thirst	see Psalms 22:15; 69:21	see John 19:28-29
Gall and vinegar offered	see Psalm 69:21	see John 19:29
Bones unbroken	see Psalm 34:20	see John 19:33,36
Heart pierced	see Psalm 22:14	see John 19:34
Side pierced	see Zechariah 12:10	see John 19:34
Looked upon	see Zechariah 12:10	see John 19:37
Buried in rich man's tomb	see Isaiah 53:9	see John 19:38-41

Psalm 22:16 also prophesied that Jesus' hands and feet would be pierced. Its recorded fulfillment is found in John 20:25. The

odds of any person other than Jesus fulfilling these prophecies are astronomical. The fulfilled prophecies in John 19 are only a small sampling of fulfilled biblical prophecies.

Could Jesus have been a fictitious character or possibly a real person whose legend grew through the centuries? Paul wrote the following verses within three to eight years of our Lord's resurrection:

> Now I make known to you, brethren, the gospel which I preached to you, which also you received, in which also you stand, by which also you are saved, if you hold fast the word which I preached to you, unless you believed in vain. For I delivered to you as of first importance what I also received, that Christ died for our sins according to the Scriptures, and that He was buried, and that He was raised on the third day according to the Scriptures, and that He appeared to Cephas, then to the twelve. After that He appeared to more than five hundred brethren at one time, most of whom remain until now, but some have fallen asleep; then He appeared to James, then to all the apostles; and last of all, as to one untimely born, He appeared to me also (1 Cor. 15:1-8).

If the resurrection hadn't actually happened, this epistle never would have survived. At the time it was written, there were too many eyewitnesses still alive, some of whom had been skeptics like Thomas. Many of the witnesses were willing to be put to death rather than disavow the claim that Jesus is the Son of God. Today's skeptic may say, "But many Muslims are willing to die for their faith as well." That statement is true—many Muslims are fanatical about what they believe—but they are not witnesses of anything. What's the difference? The eyewitnesses who saw, touched and heard Jesus didn't just believe that Jesus was crucified for our sins and resurrected in order that we may have new life in Him, but they knew for a fact it was true.

Let's get even closer to the resurrection time and listen to Peter's argument in Acts 2:22-36.

1. **Jesus the Nazarene** (see v. 22): Peter said, "Men of Israel, listen to these words: Jesus the Nazarene, a man attested to you by God" (Acts 2:22). Even at the beginning of our Lord's ministry, Philip and others like him were convinced that Jesus was the Messiah:

> Philip found Nathanael and said to him, "We have found Him of whom Moses in the Law and also the Prophets wrote— Jesus of Nazareth, the son of Joseph" (John 1:45).

> The Word became flesh, and dwelt among us (John 1:14).

> Who, although He existed in the form of God, did not regard equality with God a thing to be grasped, but emptied Himself, taking the form of a bond-servant, and being made in the likeness of men (Phil. 2:6-7).

No person can become God, but God manifested Himself in the form of a man whom we can relate to. Jesus Himself said:

If you had known Me, you would h;
My Father also; from now on you '
and have seen Him (John 14:7).

Unless you believe that I am He, you will die in
your sins (John 8:24).

2. **Attested by God** (see v. 22): Peter said to the religious leaders, "A man [Jesus] attested to you by God
with miracles and wonders and signs which God per-
formed through Him in your midst, just as you yourselves know" (Acts 2:22). Miracles (*dunamis* in Greek)
indicated a supernatural source—wonders appealed
to the imagination and signs appealed to the understanding. There are 35 separate miracles recorded in
the Gospels.

3. **A life of purpose** (see v. 23): Jesus was delivered over
to death by the predetermined plan and foreknowl-
edge of God. The Crucifixion was not a senseless
tragedy but an act of infinite kindness.

4. **The resurrection** (see vv. 24-32): Peter declared that
God raised up Jesus. He quoted Psalm 16:8-11, and
then with perfect logic showed the psalmist could
not have been talking about himself, since David's
tomb was in town.

5. **The exaltation** (see v. 33): Peter said the outpouring
of the Holy Spirit at Pentecost was evidence that
Jesus had been glorified and is now seated at the
right hand of the Father. Jesus said in John 7:37-39:

If anyone is thirsty, let him come to Me and
drink. He who believes in Me, as the Scripture said, "From his innermost being will

flow rivers of living water." But this He spoke of the Spirit, whom those who believed in Him were to receive; for the Spirit was not yet given, because Jesus was not yet glorified.

Peter pointed out that the pouring out of the Holy Spirit was something those who were present could both see and hear.

6. **Lord and Christ** (see v. 36): Peter said, "Therefore let all the house of Israel know for certain that God has made Him both Lord and Christ—this Jesus whom you crucified" (Acts 2:36). The religious leaders didn't scoff. The evidence was overwhelming and they couldn't deny it. Peter's words pierced their hearts and they asked the apostles, "Brethren, what shall we do?" (v. 37).

What should we do? We should believe and become convinced that Jesus is who He says He is and that His Word is absolutely true. We have all the evidence we need, but that alone will not be enough. Our flesh (i.e., old sinful nature) wants to rule. The god of this world will fight every decision and combat the truth with lies. I have worked with hundreds of people who profess to believe but have never fully repented. Consequently, they are not experiencing their freedom in Christ; they struggle with doubt. I also have known many who sin and confess, sin and confess, and sin again; but they don't know the truth that will set them free. Consequently, they feel guilty and are loaded with doubts because their Christianity doesn't seem to be working.

Faith is a choice. You can choose to believe or not to believe. I chose to believe God, and I have never looked back. If I hadn't chosen God, I would have had to put my confidence and faith in someone or something else, and I don't believe there is any other reliable object for my faith. That is a choice you will have to make, but understand that indecision is also a decision.

GOING DEEPER

1. What is the anchor for your soul? Why?
2. How is hope related to faith?
3. Do you have the assurance of your salvation? What is it based on?
4. If you were to die tonight and appear before God in heaven and He were to ask you, "By what right do you have the privilege to be here?" how would you answer Him?
5. How can you be assured of your salvation?
6. Share your testimony with the group or journal it.
7. Why is it necessary to have convictions?
8. Does the fulfillment of prophecy strengthen your convictions? Why or why not?
9. Why is it highly unlikely that Jesus is just a legend?
10. Why is Peter's argument so convincing?
11. Are you convinced? What would it take to convince you? Why?

lean not on your own understanding.

CERTAINTIES AND UNCERTAINTIES

*This for me will be the goal attained which has been for so long
before my soul: I shall be so completely identified with Him who has
won my heart to Himself, that I shall be like Him forever, and with
Him through all the ages to come.*

H. A. IRONSIDE

Walking by faith is a little bit like playing golf. Suppose a six-year-old boy received his first set of clubs. The little fellow teed up his ball and swang away with all his might. The furthest he hit the ball was 60 or 70 yards. He probably sprayed the ball all over the place, but let's say he was 15 degrees off target. Given the length of his drive, his ball was probably still in the fairway.

As he grew up and got a bigger set of clubs, he was able to drive the ball 150 yards. Now if his drive was still 15 degrees off target, his ball would probably be in the rough. Accuracy is even more important for golfers who drive a golf ball 300 yards off the tee. The same 15-degree deviation that allowed the little boy to remain in the fairway will send a longer drive soaring out of bounds.

Similarly, in our Christian walk, if our faith is off, our walk will be off. And if our walk is off, we need to take a good look at what we believe. Suppose at age 10 you were to begin your Christian walk 15 degrees off course. You would still be in the fairway of life, but if you continued to live that same walk for many years, life would start to get a little rough, and eventually you would find yourself out of bounds. The result is often called a midlife crisis. You thought you possessed good understanding of what constituted success, fulfillment and satisfaction, but you soon discovered that what you previously believed about life wasn't quite true. The longer you persisted in a faulty belief system, the less fulfilling and productive your daily walk would be.

Walking by faith simply means that we function in daily life on the basis of what we believe. In fact, we already walk by faith. If what we do no longer bears any fruit, then we need to change what we believe, because our misbehavior is the result of what we have chosen to believe.

FEELINGS ARE GOD'S RED FLAG OF WARNING

From birth we have been developing in our minds a means to succeed, find fulfillment, achieve satisfaction, have some fun, live in peace, and so on. Consciously or subconsciously we continue to formulate and adjust our plans for achieving these goals.

Sometimes our well-intended plans are not completely in harmony with God's plans for us. You may think, *How can I know if what I believe is right? Must I wait until I am 50 years old or until I experience some kind of midlife crisis to discover that what I believed is wrong?* Yes, we can know what is right; and no, we don't have to wait until we are 50 to find out. God designed us in such a way that we can know on a daily basis if our belief system is properly aligned with God's truth. Obviously, it must be in line with

> WHEN AN EXPERIENCE OR RELATIONSHIP LEAVES US FEELING ANGRY, ANXIOUS OR DEPRESSED, WE MAY BE CHERISHING A FAULTY GOAL, WHICH IS BASED ON A WRONG BELIEF.

what Scripture teaches, but God also has equipped us with a feedback system designed to grab our attention so that we can check the validity of our goals and desires. When an experience or relationship leaves us feeling angry, anxious or depressed, these emotional signposts are there to alert us that we may be cherishing a faulty goal, which is based on a wrong belief.

Anger Signals a Blocked Goal

When our activities, whether in a relationship or on a project, results in feelings of anger, it's usually because someone or something has blocked our goals. Something or somebody is preventing us from accomplishing what we wanted. You may have the following conviction: My goal in life is to have a loving, harmonious, happy Christian family. Who can block that goal? Every person in your family can block that goal—they not only *can*, but they *will!*

A married parent clinging to the belief that his or her sense of worth is dependent on how the family behaves will crash and burn every time his or her spouse or children fails to live up to his or her image of family harmony. The parent may become angry and controlling or a defeated victim of life's circumstances. Either option may drive family members even further away from each other.

A pastor may have the following conviction: My goal is to reach this community for Christ. Good goal? It is a wonderful desire, but if his or her sense of worth and success as a pastor hinges on that happening, the pastor will experience tremendous problems in ministry. Every person in the community can block his or her goal. Perhaps even the pastor's board members may try to block the pastor's goal. Pastors who believe their success is dependent on others will end up fighting with their boards, controlling members or quitting the ministry.

Paul wrote, "Whatever is not from faith is sin" (Rom. 14:23). In other words, if what we believe is not consistent with God's Word and will, the result is sin. For instance, somebody blocks your goal, which is based on what you believe, and you respond in an outburst of anger. That outburst of anger should prompt you to reexamine what you believe and the mental goals you have formulated to accomplish those beliefs.

Anxiety Signals an Uncertain Goal

When you feel anxious in a task or a relationship, your anxiety may be signaling your uncertainty in achieving your goal. In other words, you are hoping something will happen, but you have no guarantee it will. You can control some of the factors, but not all of them.

School

For example, a teenager believes that her happiness at school depends on her parents allowing her to attend a school dance. Not knowing how they will respond, she is anxious. If they say no, she will be angry because her goal was blocked. However, if she knows all along that there is no possible chance of their saying yes, she will be depressed because she knows her goal will not be achieved.

Depression Signals an Impossible Goal

When we base our future successes on something that can never happen, we have an impossible, hopeless goal. Our depression is a signal that our goals—no matter how spiritual or noble—may never be reached. We can be depressed for biochemical reasons; but if there is no physical cause, then depression is often rooted in a sense of hopelessness or helplessness.

A pastor was speaking at a church on the subject of depression when a woman attendee invited him and his wife to her home for dinner. The woman had been a Christian for 20 years, but her husband was not a Christian. After the pastor and his wife arrived, it didn't take long for them to realize that the real reason this woman had invited them to dinner was to help her win her husband to Christ.

The pastor later discovered that the woman had been severely depressed for many years. Her psychiatrist insisted that her depression was endogenous, which means internal or physical in its origin, and she staunchly agreed. It became evident to the pastor that her depression stemmed from an impossible goal. For 20 years she based her success and sense of worth on winning her husband and children to Christ, and on having a Christian home. She prayed for her family, witnessed to them and invited guest preachers home to dinner. She said everything she could say and did everything she could do, but to no avail. As the futility of her efforts loomed larger, her faith faltered, her hope dimmed and her depression grew.

During the dinner, the pastor struck up an enjoyable conversation with the woman's husband. He was a decent man who adequately provided for the physical needs of his family. He simply didn't see any need for God in his life. The pastor shared his testimony and tried to be a positive witness. Unfortunately, the woman's depression had negatively affected her attitude in the home, which only weakened her witness to her husband, further obliterating her goal.

We should, of course, desire that our loved ones come to Christ, praying and working to that end. But when we base our sense of worth as a Christian friend, parent or child on the salvation of our loved ones, realize that their response is beyond our ability or right to control. Witnessing is sharing our faith in the power of the Holy Spirit and leaving the results to God. We can't save anyone. Depression often signals that we are desperately clinging to a goal we have little or no chance of achieving, which is not a healthy goal.

There Are Wrong Responses to People or Things That Frustrate Goals

If our goals can be blocked or are uncertain, how do we respond to someone or something that threatens our plans? We may attempt to control or manipulate people or circumstances that stand between us and our achievements.

For example, a pastor's goal is to have the finest youth ministry in the community. However, one of his board members attempts to block his goal by insisting that a music ministry is more important. Every attempt by the pastor to hire a youth pastor is vetoed by the influential board member who first wants to hire a music director. The pastor believes that his sense of worth and success in ministry is on the line; therefore, he shifts into power mode to push the stumbling block out of the way. He lobbies his cause with other board members. He solicits support from denominational leaders. He preaches on the importance of youth ministry to gain congregational support. He looks for ways to change the opposition's mind or remove him from the board, because he believes that his success in ministry is dependent on reaching his goal of having a great youth ministry.

Consider the goal of a mother who believes that her sense of worth depends on how well her children turn out: Her goal is to raise perfect little Christians who will become doctors and lawyers. Yet as her children reach their teens and begin to express their independence, their behavior doesn't always match her ideal. She is heading for a collision because her children want their freedom and she wants to control them. She feels she must control their behavior, because she believes her success as a mother depends on it. If they don't attend the functions she wants them to attend, they can't go anywhere. If they don't listen to the music she expects them to listen to, they lose their radio and TV privileges. Somewhere in her journey she never heard that parenting is an 18-year process of letting go, and the fruit of the Spirit is self-control, not child control.

It is not hard to understand why some people manipulate circumstances or control others. Their identity is completely wrapped up in other people and their circumstances. This is a false belief, as evidenced by the fact that the most insecure people you will ever meet are manipulators and controllers.

People who cannot control those who frustrate their goals will probably respond with bitterness, anger or resentment. Or they may simply resort to a martyr's complex, which was the case for the woman whose husband wouldn't come to Christ. She had been unsuccessful at getting him into the Kingdom, so her faith and hope shriveled into depression. She was resigned to bearing her cross of hopelessness and hanging on until the Lord's return. Unless she adjusts her goals, she will live the rest of her life in defeat.

Does God Give Bad or Unachievable Goals?

Consider this faith-stretching question: If God wants something done, can it be done? In other words, if God has a goal for your life, can it be blocked? Is its fulfillment uncertain or impossible?

No God-given goal for your life can ever be impossible, uncertain or blocked. You will never hear God say in effect, "I've called you into existence, I've made you My child and I have something for you to do. I know you won't be able to do it, but give it your best shot." That's ludicrous! It's like saying to your child, "I want you to mow the lawn. Unfortunately, the lawn is full of rocks, the mower doesn't work, and there's no gas. But give it your best shot anyway." When an authority figure issues a command that cannot be obeyed, it undermines the authority of the leader in the minds of those who are in positions of submission.

God had a seemingly impossible goal for a young maid named Mary. An angel told her that she would bear a son while still a virgin and that her son would be the Savior of the world. When she inquired about this seemingly impossible feat, the angel simply said, "Nothing will be impossible with God" (Luke 1:37).

You wouldn't give your child a task he or she couldn't possibly complete, and God doesn't assign goals you can't achieve. His goals for you are possible, certain and achievable. You need to understand what His goal for your life is and then say as Mary said, "Behold, the bondslave of the Lord; may it be done to me according to your word" (Luke 1:38).

What Is the Difference Between Goals and Desires?

In order to live a successful life, we need to distinguish a godly goal from a godly desire. For us as Christians, this liberating distinction can spell the difference between success and failure, inner peace and inner pain.

> A godly goal is any specific orientation that reflects God's purpose for your life and does not depend on people or circumstances beyond your ability or right to control.

Whom do you have the ability and right to control? No one can block that goal but yourself. The only person who can render it uncertain or impossible is yourself. If you adopt the attitude of Mary and cooperate with God, your goal can be reached.

> A godly desire is any specific result that depends on the cooperation of other people or the success of events or favorable circumstances, which you have no ability or right to control.

You cannot base your success or sense of worth on your desires, no matter how godly they may be, because you cannot control their fulfillment. Some of your desires will be blocked, remain uncertain and eventually prove to be impossible. Let's face it, life doesn't always go your way, and many of your desires will not be met.

We will struggle with anger, anxiety and depression when we elevate a desire to a goal in our own minds. But by comparison, when a desire isn't met, we will only face disappointment. Life is full of disappointments and we must learn to live with them. Dealing with the disappointments of unmet desires is a lot easier than dealing with the anger, anxiety and depression caused by goals based on wrong beliefs.

Does God make a distinction between a goal and a desire? Yes, He does. God says:

> "For I have no pleasure in the death of anyone who dies," declares the Lord GOD. "Therefore, repent and live" (Ezek. 18:32).

It is God's desire that everyone repent and live, but not everyone will. John writes: "My little children, I am writing these things to you so that you may not sin" (1 John 2:1). Certainly the integrity, sovereignty and success of God are not dependent on whether we sin or not. God has no blocked goals. But it is God's *desire* that everyone repent, even though not everyone will.

Does God have any genuine goals—specific results that cannot be blocked? Praise the Lord, yes! For example, Jesus Christ will return and take us home to heaven to be with Him forever—it will happen. Satan will be cast into the abyss for eternity—count on it. Rewards will be distributed to the saints for their faithfulness—look forward to it. Remember, God's goals are not desires that can be thwarted by the fickle nature of a fallen humanity. What God has determined to do, He will do.

When you begin to align your goals with God's goals and your desires with God's desires, you will rid your life of a lot of anger, anxiety and depression. The homemaker who wants a happy, harmonious family is expressing a godly desire, but she cannot guarantee it will happen. Her goal is to become the wife and mother God wants her to be. Only she can block that goal for her life—no one else.

She may object, "But what if my husband has a midlife crisis or my children rebel?" Problems do not and will not block her goal to be the wife and mother God calls her to be. Such trials will surely test her faith. If anything, difficulties in the family should further encourage her commitment. It is in these times of trouble when her husband truly needs a godly wife and her children a godly mother. Family difficulties should refine her goal of being the woman God wants her to be.

The pastor whose success and sense of worth are based on his goal to win his community to Christ, to have the best youth ministry in town or to increase giving to missions by 50 percent is headed for a fall. These are worthwhile desires, but no pastor should deem himself a success or failure based on whether or not he achieves them. His goal should be to become the pastor God called him to be. No member of his church or community can block that goal.

What Is the Ultimate Goal?

God's goal for your life is that you become the person He created you to be. Sanctification is God's will (i.e., goal) for your life (see 1 Thess. 4:3). Nobody and nothing on Earth can keep you

> WITNESSING IS SHARING OUR FAITH IN THE POWER OF THE HOLY SPIRIT AND LEAVING THE RESULTS TO GOD. WE CAN'T SAVE ANYONE.

from being the person God called you to be. You need to understand that a lot of distractions, diversions, disappointments, trials, temptations and traumas will come along to try to disrupt the process. Every day you will struggle against the world, the flesh and the devil, each of which are opposed to your success at being who God wants you to be.

Paul teaches that the tribulations we face are actually a means of achieving our supreme goal of conforming to the image of God:

> We also exult in our tribulations, knowing that tribulation brings about perseverance; and perseverance, proven character; and proven character, hope; and hope does not disappoint, because the love of God has been poured out within our hearts through the Holy Spirit who was given to us (Rom. 5:3-5).

James offers similar counsel:

> Consider it all joy, my brethren, when you encounter various trials, knowing that the testing of your faith produces endurance. And let endurance have its perfect result, so that you may be perfect and complete, lacking in nothing (Jas. 1:2-4).

The word "exult" means to heighten joy. To be under tribulation means to be under pressure, and to persevere means to remain under pressure. Persevering through tribulations results in proven character, which is God's goal for us.

Imagine a Christian wife who asked for help because her husband had just left her. What kind of hope could we give her? We could say, "Don't worry; we'll win him back." That is a legitimate desire but the wrong goal, which could lead to manipulation and control. Attempts to manipulate him to come back may be the same kind of controlling behavior that caused him to leave in the first place. It would be better to say:

> I will help you work through this crisis (persevere) to become the person God wants you to be (proven charac-

ter). If you haven't committed yourself to be the wife and mother God has called you to be, would you now? You can't change him, but you can change yourself, which is the best way to win him back anyway. Even if he doesn't come back, you can come through this crisis with proven character. That is where your hope lies.

She may rightly ask, "What if the problem is 90 percent his fault?" She doesn't have any control over that. By committing to change herself, she is responsibly dealing with what *she* can control. Her transformation may be just the motivation her husband needs to change himself and restore their relationship.

Trials and tribulations reveal wrong goals, but they can be the catalyst for achieving God's ultimate goal for our lives—our sanctification. Sanctification is the process of conforming to His image. It's during these times of pressure when our emotions raise their warning flags, signaling blocked, uncertain or impossible goals, which are based on our desires instead of on God's goal of proven character.

Some defeated spouses say, "My marriage is hopeless," and then try to "solve" the problem by changing partners. If they think their first marriage was hopeless, they should be aware that second marriages fail at a far higher rate. Others feel their jobs or churches are hopeless, so they change jobs or churches, only to discover that their new job or church is just as hopeless. In most cases, they should hang in there, at least until they grow up. There are legitimate times to change jobs or churches, but if they are running from their own immaturity, it surely will follow them wherever they go.

A suit salesman heard this message about God's goal for his life and it changed him. He shared that he had been an angry suit salesman. His Jewish boss had to set him aside a number of times because of his temper. The salesman had a personal goal to sell so many suits each week, and it angered him when he didn't meet his goal or talk a customer into buying a suit. In the past, he hounded customers and manipulated sales, but he soon realized he had the wrong goal. After hearing the truth, he decided to become the suit salesman God had called him to be. It had such an effect on him that his boss asked him after a week if he was all right. The anger had dissipated. He started to consider each customer to be more important than himself (see Phil. 2:1-5). To his surprise, he sold more suits than he ever had before.

Is there an easier way to conform to God's image other than enduring tribulations? Probably every one of us, as believers, has looked for one, but it is usually the difficult times of testing that bring about the maturity that makes life meaningful. We need occasional mountaintop experiences, but the fertile soil for growth is always down in the valleys, not on the mountaintops. Paul says, "The goal of our instruction is love" (1 Tim. 1:5). Love (agape) is the character of God, because God is love (see 1 John 4:7-8). If striving for godly character is our primary goal, then we will bear the fruit of the Spirit—love, joy (instead of depression), peace (instead of anxiety) and patience (instead of anger) (see Gal. 5:22-23). The following poem from an unknown author expresses well the message of this chapter:

"Disappointments—His appointment,"
    Change one letter, then I see
That the thwarting of my purpose
    Is God's better choice for me.
His appointment must be blessing,
    Tho' it may come in disguise,
For the end from the beginning
    Open to His wisdom lies.

"Disappointment—His appointment,"
    No good will He withhold,
From denials oft we gather
    treasures of His love untold.
Well He knows each broken purpose
    Leads to fuller, deeper trust,
And the end of all His dealings
    Proves our God is wise and just.

"Disappointments—His appointment,"
    Lord, I take it, then, as such,
Like clay in hands of a potter,
    Yielding wholly to Thy touch.
My life's plan is Thy molding;
    Not one single choice be mine;
Let me answer, unrepining—
    "Father, not my will, but Thine."

GOING DEEPER

1. How do anger, anxiety and depression relate to what you think and believe?
2. What goals do you have or have you had that can be blocked, uncertain or impossible?
3. What is your natural tendency when your plans or goals are threatened?
4. Why does the attempt to control others or manipulate circumstances signify insecurity?
5. What is wrong with someone's basic belief system when they control or manipulate?
6. What are the key differences between goals and desires?
7. What is God's primary goal for your life?

8. What has God already accomplished, and what do you need to do in order to be useful and fruitful?

9. Consider the following parable:

There was a man who was asleep in his cabin when he was suddenly awakened. The Savior appeared in his room and it was filled with light. The Lord said, "I have work for you to do." He showed him a large rock, and told him to push against that rock with all his might. This the man did, and for many days he toiled from sun up to sun down; his shoulder set squarely against the cold massive surface of the rock pushing with all his might. Each night the man returned to his cabin sore and worn out, wondering if his whole day had been spent in vain.

Seeing that the man was showing signs of discouragement, Satan decided to enter the picture, placing thoughts in the man's mind, such as, *Why kill yourself over this, you're never going to move it. Boy! You've been at it a long time and you haven't even scratched the surface.* The man began to get the impression that the task was impossible and that he was an unworthy servant because he wasn't able to move the massive stone.

These thoughts discouraged and disheartened him, and he started to ease up his efforts. *Why kill myself?* he thought. *I'll just put in my time, expending a minimum amount of effort and that will be good enough.* And that he did, or at least planned on doing until one day he decided to take his troubles to the Lord. "Lord," he said, "I have labored hard and long in your service, putting forth all my strength to do that which you have asked me. Yet, after all this time, I have not even nudged that rock half a millimeter. What is wrong? Am I failing you?"

"My son, when long ago I asked you to serve me and you accepted, I told you to push against the rock with all your strength. That you have done. But never once did I mention that I expected you to move it, at least, not by yourself! Your task was to push! Now you come to me all discouraged thinking that you have failed and ready to quit. But is that really so? Look at yourself. Your arms are strong and muscled; your back sinewed and brown. Your hands are callused and your legs have become massive and hard. Through opposition you have grown much and your ability now far surpasses that which you used to have. Yet still, you haven't succeeded in moving the rock; and you come to me now with a heavy heart and your strength spent. I, my son, will move the rock. Your calling was to be and to push, and to exercise your faith and trust in my wisdom, and this you have done."[1]

Faith Appraisal

Before you read the next chapter, evaluate your faith by completing the following Faith Appraisal. Give serious thought to the sentence completions.

Faith Appraisal

	Low				High

1. How successful am I?   1   2   3   4   5
   I would be more successful if _____.

2. How significant am I?   1   2   3   4   5
   I would be more significant if _____.

3. How fulfilled am I?   1   2   3   4   5
   I would be more fulfilled if _____.

4. How satisfied am I?   1   2   3   4   5
   I would be more satisfied if _____.

5. How happy am I?   1   2   3   4   5
   I would be happier if _____.

6. How much fun am I
   having?   1   2   3   4   5
   I would have more fun if _____.

7. How secure am I?   1   2   3   4   5
   I would be more secure if _____.

8. How peaceful am I?   1   2   3   4   5
   I would have more peace if _____.

ON THE
RIGHT PATH

*Faith is a living, daring confidence in God's grace. It is so sure and
certain that a man could stake his life on it a thousand times.*

MARTIN LUTHER

At the end of the last chapter, you were encouraged to complete the
Faith Appraisal. How you completed the sentences: "I would be
more successful if . . . ", "I would be more significant if . . . ",
and so on reflect what you presently believe. You are right now living by faith according to what you believe. Assuming that your
basic physiological needs—food, shelter and safety—are met, you
are most likely motivated to live a successful, significant, fulfilled,
satisfied, happy, fun, secure and peaceful life. Living a full life is

perfectly fine, because God hasn't called you to be an insecure, insignificant, unfulfilled failure. However, chances are you may not have the same definition for these eight faith qualities of life that God does. Consequently, you are not living up to your God-given potential.

In this chapter, you and I are going to further explore the eight subjects addressed in the Faith Appraisal. Ranked from one to five—lowest to highest—your responses can potentially all be fives. This is dependent on what you believe, not on others or the circumstances of life. If your responses were all ones, it means your faith can only grow from here.

Each of the eight subjects is related to a key concept. The following chart summarizes each subject and its key concept.

Success
Key Concept: Goals
Success is accepting God's goal for our lives and becoming what He has called us to be by His grace (see Josh. 1:7-8; 2 Pet. 1:3-10, 3 John 2).

Significance
Key Concept: Time
What is forgotten in time is of little significance. What is remembered for eternity is of greatest significance (see Acts 5:33-40; 1 Cor. 3:13; 1 Tim. 4:7-8).

Fulfillment
Key Concept: Role Preference
Fulfillment is discovering our own uniqueness in Christ and using our gifts to build up others and to glorify the Lord (see Matt. 25:14-30; Rom. 12:1-18; 2 Tim. 4:5).

Satisfaction
Key Concept: Quality
Satisfaction is living righteously and seeking to raise the quality of the relationships, services and products we're involved with (see Prov. 18:24; Matt. 5:5; 2 Tim. 4:7).

Happiness
Key Concept: Appreciating What We Have
Happiness is being thankful for what we do have, rather than focusing on what we don't have—because happy are the people who appreciate what they have (see Phil. 4:12; 1 Thess. 5:18; 1 Tim. 6:6-8)!

Fun
Key Concept: Uninhibited Spontaneity
The secret to fun is to remove unbiblical blocks such as keeping up appearances (see 2 Sam. 6:20-23; Rom. 14:22; Gal. 1:10; 5:1).

Security
Key Concept: Relating to the Eternal
Insecurity comes when we depend on things that pass away rather than on things that last forever (see John 10:27-30; Rom. 8:31-39; Eph. 1:13-14).

Peace
Key Concept: Establishing Internal Order
The peace of God is internal, not external (see Isa. 32:17; Jer. 6:14; John 14:27; Phil. 4:6-7).

GOD'S GUIDELINES FOR THE WALK OF FAITH

Success

Key Concept: Goals

A troubled woman who had many moral lapses made an appointment to see her pastor. She quoted 3 John 2: "Beloved, I pray that in all respects you may prosper and be in good health." Then she said, "If God has promised prosperity, success and good health, why am I not experiencing them?" She had failed to read the whole verse, which read, "Just as your soul prospers." She was experiencing about as much success as her soul was.

> WE CAN BE A COMPLETE FAILURE IN THE EYES OF THIS WORLD BUT SUCCESSFUL IN GOD'S EYES.

Bear in mind that we can be a complete failure in the eyes of this world but successful in God's eyes. Conversely, we can be successful in this world but a complete failure for all eternity. Success is related to goals, and each of our goals are not always the same. If you rated yourself low in the success category, you are probably having difficulty reaching your goals in life. If you aren't reaching your goals, it may be because you are not working on the right goals.

Yet there is one universal goal for everyone:

His divine power has granted to us everything pertaining to life and godliness, through the true knowledge of Him who called us by His own glory and excellence. For by these He has granted to us His precious and magnificent promises, so that by them you may become partakers of the divine nature, having escaped the corruption that is in the world by lust.

Now for this very reason also, applying all diligence, in your faith supply moral excellence, and in your moral excellence, knowledge, and in your knowledge, self-control, and in your self-control, perseverance, and in your perseverance, godliness, and in your godliness, brotherly kindness, and in your brotherly kindness, love. For if these qualities are yours and are increasing, they render you neither useless nor unfruitful in the true knowledge of our Lord Jesus Christ. For he who lacks these qualities is blind or short-sighted, having forgotten his purification from his former sins. Therefore, brethren, be all the more diligent to make certain about His calling and choosing you; for as long as you practice these things, you will never stumble (2 Pet. 1:3-10).

Notice that God's goal begins with who we are on the basis of what God has already done for us. He has given us "life and godliness." We are forgiven and on the path of sanctification (i.e., conforming to the image of God). We already are partakers of the divine nature, having escaped sin's corruption. What a great start!

Our primary job now is to diligently adopt God's character goals—moral excellence, knowledge, self-control, perseverance, godliness, brotherly kindness and Christian love—and apply them to our lives. Focusing on God's goals will lead to ultimate success—success in God's terms. Peter promises that as these qualities increase in our lives through practice, we will be useful and fruitful, and we will never stumble. That is a legitimate basis for a true sense of worth and success. Nobody can keep us from accomplishing it!

Notice that this list does not mention talents, intelligence or gifts, which are not equally distributed to all believers. Our identity and sense of worth aren't determined by those qualities; rather, our identities are based in Christ and our growth in character, both of which are equally accessible to every Christian. Those Christians who are not committed to God's goals for character are sad stories of failure. According to Peter, they have forgotten their purification from former sins. They have forgotten who they are in Christ.

Another helpful perspective on success can be found in Joshua's experience of leading the Israelites into the Promised Land. God said to him:

> Be strong and very courageous; be careful to do according to all the law which Moses My servant commanded you; do not turn from it to the right or to the left, so that you may have success wherever you go. This book of the law shall not depart from your mouth, but you shall meditate on it day and night, so that you may be careful to do according to all that is written in it; for then you will make your way prosperous, and then you will have success (Josh. 1:7-8).

Was Joshua's success dependent on other people or on favorable circumstances? No. Success hinged entirely on living according to God's Word. If Joshua would believe what God had said and do what God had told him to do, he would succeed. Sounds simple enough, but God immediately put Joshua to the test by giving him a rather unorthodox battle plan for conquering Jericho. Marching around the city for seven days and then blowing a horn wasn't exactly an approved military tactic in Joshua's day—nor is it in our day!

Joshua's success was conditional on his obeying God, regardless of how foolish His plan seemed. As Joshua 6 records, Joshua's success had nothing to do with the circumstances of the battle but everything to do with obedience. Success is accepting God's goal for our lives, and by His grace, becoming what He has called us to be.

Significance

Key Concept: Time

Significance is a time concept. What is forgotten in time is of little significance. What is remembered for eternity is of great significance. Paul wrote to the Corinthians: "If any man's work . . . remains, he will receive a reward" (1 Cor. 3:14). He instructed Timothy: "Discipline yourself for the purpose of godliness . . . since it holds promise for the present life and also for the life to come" (1 Tim. 4:7-8). If we want to increase our significance, focus our energies on significant activities—those which will remain for eternity.

Have each of us thought about what the world considers significant and how it compares to God's Word? Super Bowls and World Cups capture the headlines, but who won 25 years ago? Who really cares? Teenagers think a rock concert is significant, but where will the band be 20 years from now? We keep records and build memorials, but within a generation the deeds have been outdone and the memories fade.

The Christian, on the other hand, is doing Kingdom work that will last forever. Some of us may feel insignificant teaching third graders at church, but we are teaching the truth to young children. What they choose to believe will have eternal consequences. The nursery may seem like a small thing, but it frees up moms and dads to worship God and receive instruction. There are no insignificant children of God, and there are no insignificant tasks in the kingdom of God.

Fulfillment

Key Concept: Role Preference

Fulfillment is realized when we bloom where we're planted. Peter wrote: "As each one has received a special gift, employ it in serving one another" (1 Pet. 4:10). Fulfillment is discovering our own uniqueness in Christ and using our gifts and talents to edify others and to glorify the Lord.

An aerospace engineer had just received the Lord. He knew God wanted him to be an ambassador for Christ on the job, so he started a breakfast Bible study in the bowling alley next door to the office. The Bible study announcement had only been posted in the office about a hour when a Jewish fellow pulled it off the wall and brought it to the engineer. "You can't bring Jesus in here," he objected.

"I can't do otherwise," responded the engineer. "Every day I walk in here Jesus comes in with me." The not-yet Christian wasn't impressed with his response!

One of the men who found Christ through the Bible study became a powerful witness at the plant. He passed out tracts everywhere he went. When the engineer left the aerospace firm to enter the seminary, the new convert took over the Bible study.

A few months later, the seminarian visited his friends in the Bible study. "Do you remember the Jewish fellow?" the leader asked.

"Sure, I remember him," recalled the engineer. How could he forget the man's brash opposition to the Bible study?

"Well, he got sick and almost died. I went to the hospital and visited him every night. I thought you would like to know that I led him to the Lord." The ex-engineer became a spiritual grandparent that day. It all began when he started a simple Bible study at his office in order to do what Paul wrote: "Do the work of an evangelist, fulfill your ministry" (2 Tim. 4:5).

God has a unique place of ministry for you. It is important to your sense of fulfillment that you realize your calling in life. The key is to discover the roles you occupy in which you cannot be replaced, and then decide to be what God wants you to be in those roles. For example, of the 6 billion people in the world, you are the only one who occupies your unique role as husband, father, wife, mother, parent or child in your home. God has specially planted you to serve Him by serving your family in that environment.

Furthermore, you are the only one who knows your neighbors as you do. You also occupy a unique role as an ambassador for Christ where you work. These are your mission fields, and you are the worker God has appointed for the harvest there. Your greatest fulfillment will come from accepting and occupying God's unique place for you to the best of your ability. Sadly, so many people miss their calling in life by looking for fulfillment in the world. Find your fulfillment in the kingdom of God by deciding to be an ambassador for Christ in the world (see 2 Cor. 5:20).

Satisfaction

Key Concept: Quality

Satisfaction comes from living righteously and seeking to raise the level of quality in your relationships, service and product. Jesus said, "Blessed are those who hunger and thirst for righteousness, for they shall be satisfied" (Matt. 5:6). Do you believe that? If you do, what would you be doing? You would be hungering and thirsting after righteousness. If you aren't doing that, then you really don't believe it.

What causes you to become dissatisfied with someone or something? Ask people when they have become dissatisfied. Inevitably they identify a time when the quality of a relationship, service or work diminished.

Satisfaction is a quality issue, not a quantity issue. You will achieve greater satisfaction from doing a few things well than from doing many things haphazardly or hastily. The key to personal satisfaction is not found in broadening the scope of your activities but in deepening them through a commitment to quality.

> # SATISFACTION IS A QUALITY ISSUE, NOT A QUANTITY ISSUE.

The same is true in relationships. If you are dissatisfied in your relationships, perhaps you have spread yourself too thin. Solomon wrote, "A man of too many friends comes to ruin, but there is a friend who sticks closer than a brother" (Prov. 18:24). Satisfaction comes from having a few quality friends who are committed to meaningful relationships with one another.

That is what our Lord modeled for us. He taught the multitudes and He equipped 70 for ministry, but He invested most of His time in the twelve disciples. Out of those Twelve, He selected three—Peter, James and John—to be with Him on the Mount of Transfiguration, on the Mount of Olives and in the Garden of Gethsemane. While suffering on the cross, Jesus committed the care of His mother to John (see John 19:26-27). Those were quality relationships, and we all need the satisfaction that quality relationships bring.

Happiness
Key Concept: Appreciating What We Have
The world's concept of happiness is getting what we want. Madison Avenue tells us we need a flashier car, a sexier cologne or any number of items that are better, faster and easier to use

than what we already have. We watch commercials and read ads, and we become antsy to get all the latest fashions, fads and fancy doodads. We're not really happy until we get what we want.

In today's consumer mentality, true happiness is summed up in the simple phrase "Happy are those who want what they have." As long as we focus on what we don't have, we'll be unhappy. But when we begin to appreciate what we already have, we'll be happy all our lives. Paul wrote: "Godliness with contentment is great gain. For we brought nothing into the world, and we can take nothing out of it. But if we have food and clothing, we will be content with that" (1 Tim. 6:6-8, *NIV*).

Actually, we already have everything we need to make us happy forever. We have Christ. We have eternal life. We are loved by a heavenly Father who has promised to supply all our needs. No wonder the Bible commands us to be thankful (see 1 Thess. 5:18). If we really want to be happy, we need to learn to be content with life and thankful for what we already have in Christ.

Fun

Key Concept: Uninhibited Spontaneity

Fun is uninhibited spontaneity. Have you ever planned a major event? Chances are the last time you really had fun it was spontaneous—you threw off your inhibitions. Worldly people know they need to get rid of their inhibitions in order to have fun.

The secret to enjoying uninhibited spontaneity as a Christian is to remove unscriptural inhibitors. Chief among the inhibitors of Christian fun is our fleshly tendency to keep up appearances. We don't want to look out of place or be thought of less by others, so we stifle our spontaneity with a form of false decorum—pleasing people. Paul wrote that those who live to please people are not serving Christ (see Gal. 1:10). Their joyless cry is, "What will people say?" The liberated in Christ respond, "Who cares what people say? I care what God says, and I stopped

playing for the grandstand a long time ago when I started playing for the coach."

I love the uninhibited joy of King David. He was so happy
about returning the Ark to Jerusalem that he leaped and danced
before the Lord in celebration (see 2 Sam. 6:12-15). He knew there
was joy in the presence of God. But Michal, his party-pooping
wife, thought his behavior was unbecoming to a king, and she
told him so in no uncertain terms (see v. 20). David said, "Too
bad for you, lady. I'm dancing before the Lord, not you or anybody else. And I'm going to keep dancing whether you like it or
not" (see v. 21). As it turned out, Michal was the person God
judged in the incident, not David (see v. 23). It is a lot more fun
to please the Lord than to try to please people.

Security
Key Concept: Relating to the Eternal

Insecurity stems from dependence upon temporal things, which
we have no right or ability to control. Do you realize that God is
shaking the foundations of this world? Insecurity is a global
problem. There are going to be some tough days ahead for this
fallen world. It doesn't take a genius to figure that out.

Our security can only be found in the eternal life of Christ.
Jesus said no one can snatch us out of His hand (see John 10:27-
29). Paul declared that nothing can separate us from the love of
God in Christ (see Rom. 8:35-39) and that we are sealed in Him
by the Holy Spirit (see Eph. 1:13-14). How much more secure can
we get than that? Every "thing" we now have we shall someday
lose. Jim Elliot said, "He is no fool to give up that which he cannot keep in order to gain that which he cannot lose."[1] Paul wrote:

> But whatever things were gain to me, those things I have
> counted as loss for the sake of Christ. More than that, I
> count all things to be loss in view of the surpassing value

of knowing Christ Jesus my Lord, for whom I have suffered the loss of all things, and count them but rubbish so that I may gain Christ (Phil. 3:7-8).

Peace

Key Concept: Establishing Internal Order

Peace on Earth, goodwill toward men. Isn't that what everybody wants? It is a great desire but the wrong goal. Nobody can guarantee external peace, because nobody can control people or circumstances. Nations sign and break peace treaties with frightening regularity. One group of peace marchers confronts a group of activists, and they end up beating each other over the head with their placards. Couples lament that there would be peace in their home "if only my spouse would shape up."

> NOTHING WILL HAPPEN
> TO YOU TODAY THAT YOU
> CANNOT HANDLE WITH GOD
> BY YOUR SIDE.

The peace of God *is* internal, not external. Peace *with* God is something you already have (see Rom. 5:1). The peace *of* God is something you need to appropriate daily in your inner person. You can have the internal peace of God in the midst of storms that rage in the external world (see John 14:27). A lot of things can disrupt your external world, because you *can't* control all of your circumstances and relationships. However, you *can* control the inner world of your thoughts and emotions by allowing the peace of God to rule in your heart on a daily basis. Chaos may encircle you, but God is bigger than any storm. Nothing will happen to you today that you cannot handle with God by your side. Personal worship, prayer and interaction with God's Word will enable you to experience the peace of God (see Phil 4:6-7; Col. 3:15-16).

The nonbeliever may say, "Well, I suppose that's true, but I still believe . . . " What will they decide to live by—what they mentally acknowledge as true or what they still believe? Always the latter—*always*! Walking by faith is simply choosing to believe what God says is true and living accordingly by the power of the Holy Spirit. May the good Lord enable you to do so.

MOTIVATION FOR THE LIFE OF FAITH

May these words motivate you to live by faith as it has me:

I am part of the "fellowship of the unashamed." I have Holy Spirit power. The die has been cast. I've stepped over the line. The decision has been made. I am a disciple of His. I won't look back, let up, slow down, back away or be still. My past is redeemed, my present makes sense and my future is secure. I am finished and done with low living, sight walking, small planning, smooth knees, colorless dreams, tame visions, mundane talking, chintzy giving and dwarfed goals!

I no longer need preeminence, prosperity, position, promotions, plaudits or popularity. I don't have to be right, first, tops, recognized, praised, regarded or rewarded. I now live by presence, learn by faith, love by patience, lift by prayer and labor by power.

My face is set, my gait is fast, my goal is heaven, my road is narrow, my way is rough, my companions few, my guide reliable, my mission clear. I cannot be bought, compromised, detoured, lured away, turned back, diluted or delayed. I will not flinch in the face of sacrifice, hesitate in the presence of adversity, negotiate at the table of the enemy, ponder at the pool of popularity or meander in the maze of mediocrity.

I won't give up, shut up, let up or burn up till I've preached up, prayed up, paid up, stored up and stayed up for the cause of Christ.

I am a disciple of Jesus. I must go till He comes, give till I drop, preach till all know and work till He stops.

And when He comes to get His own, He'll have no problems recognizing me. My colors will be clear.[2]

GOING DEEPER

1. Do you believe that you can be a successful politician, businessperson, scientist or other professional and live consistently with God's Word? Why or why not?
2. What does our success as Christians depend on?
3. What does the world consider significant, which in light of eternity is insignificant?
4. How can you live a more fulfilled life?
5. Can anything the flesh craves ever be satisfied?
6. What satisfies and continues to satisfy you?
7. How can you be truly happy in this world?
8. Fun may be fleeting, but the joy of the Lord lasts forever. How can you experience the joy of the Lord and make your Christian experience more fun?
9. What causes you to feel insecure?
10. How can you be more secure?
11. How do goals and desires relate to the possibility of experiencing inner peace?
12. What kind of peace can you have and how do you get it?

DOUBT AND
MENTAL HEALTH

*The doubter's dissatisfaction with his doubt is as great and
widespread as the doubt itself.*

JAN DEWITT

I'm afraid I'll lose control. I'm afraid of my father, of
God, of what people will think of me. I'm afraid "it" will
catch up with me. I'm afraid my parents will embarrass
me. I'm afraid I'll embarrass myself. My heart will stop.
I'm afraid I'll throw up in front of everybody, and people
will talk about me. I'm afraid I'll jump off the balcony.
I'm afraid I'll die. I'm afraid I won't. I'm not good

enough for my friends. I'm not good enough for God. I'll be found out. I'm afraid of the shadows on the wall. Someone's right outside my window waiting. I'm afraid of myself. I'm not talented enough. I'm not pretty enough. I'll panic. I won't get everything done. I'll choke. I'm inadequate. I'm afraid I'll go crazy. I'm afraid they will lock me up and no one will care anymore. They won't like me if they really know me. My heart will be broken. I'm not rich enough. I'm not strong enough. No one [would] ever be able to love me if they really knew me. I'm afraid to be myself. I'm afraid I have no self. I'm afraid I might fail. What if I succeed? What if it doesn't happen? What if it does? Why am I so afraid?[1]

Such are the thoughts of a person who doubts everything. This was called doubting mania the first half of the last century. It was described as an extreme self-consciousness and preoccupation with hesitation and doubt. Today the diagnosis would be anxiety disorder and/or obsessive-compulsive disorder. Anxiety disorders are the number one mental health problem in the world, followed by depression, which is the common cold of mental illness. Depression is often the result of having struggled with obsessive worry and doubt.

Obsessive doubters have more of a mental struggle than a behavioral problem. In other words, they are more obsessive than compulsive. The mental obsession is usually regarding issues that can't be proved to their satisfaction. Rather than make the choice to believe and live accordingly by faith, they are limited in what they can do by their uncertainties.

The Bible is certainly not silent about such mental problems. The Old Testament records, "Elijah came near to all the people and said, 'How long will you hesitate between two opinions? If the LORD is God, follow Him; but if Baal, follow him'"

(1 Kings 18:21). In the New Testament, James writes:

> But if any of you lacks wisdom, let him ask of God, who gives to all generously and without reproach, and it will be given to him. But he must ask in faith without any doubting, for the one who doubts is like the surf of the sea, driven and tossed by the wind. For that man ought not to expect that he will receive anything from the Lord, being a double-minded man, unstable in all his ways (1:5-8).

Such verses are a challenge for most of us, but they only increase the anxiety when read by people who have obsessive thoughts. *Have I believed enough? Did I ask in faith? Does God hear me? Am I a Christian?* The personal misery of living in doubt is probably worse than the frustration of living with those who do. Hence, the doubter's dissatisfaction with his doubt is as great and widespread as the doubt itself.

Resolving such mental health problems is beyond the scope of this book, but I have dealt with anxiety disorders in *Freedom from Fear* (Harvest House Publishers, 1999), depression in *Finding Hope Again* (Regal Books, 1999) and a poor self-image due to a lack of understanding who you are in Christ in *Overcoming Negative Self-Image* (Regal Books, 2003). I will deal more with the spiritual battle for the mind in the next chapter. For the rest of this chapter, I will draw from these resources and share some key points in dealing with doubt and mental health.

IDENTITY AND SENSE OF WORTH

After 30-plus years of working with people, I have found one common denominator among Christians that I have counseled, regardless of their problem: They did not know who they were in

Christ, nor did they understand what it meant to be children of God. Where was the inner sense of "Abba! Father!" (Gal. 4:6)? If the Holy Spirit bears witness with our spirit that we are children of God (see Rom. 8:16), then why were my counselees not sensing it? To be spiritually alive means that our inner selves or souls are united with God. We have become temples of God because His Spirit dwells within us (see Rom. 8:10-11).

Spiritual life—our union with God—is most commonly portrayed in the New Testament as being in Christ. For every verse that says Christ is in us, there are 10 verses that teach we are in Christ or in Him. The fact that every true believer is alive in Christ is Paul's fundamental teaching:

> For this reason I have sent to you Timothy, who is my beloved and faithful child in the Lord, and he will remind you of my ways which are *in Christ*, just as I teach everywhere in every church (1 Cor. 4:17, emphasis added).

Paul taught that Christ would meet all of our needs according to His riches in glory (see Phil. 4:19). The primary needs are the "being" needs, such as life itself, identity, acceptance, security and significance. What Adam and Eve lost in the fall was life, and what Jesus came to give us was life (see John 10:10). We probably have tried or still try to make a name for ourselves in this fallen world, "But as many as received Him, to them He gave the right to become children of God, even to those who believe in His name" (John 1:12). "See how great a love the Father has bestowed on us, that we would be called children of God; and such we are" (1 John 3:1). Carefully read the following verses and see how our needs for acceptance, security and significance already have been met:

In Christ

I Am Accepted in Christ

John 1:12	I am God's child.
John 15:15	I am Christ's friend.
Romans 5:1	I have been justified.
1 Corinthians 6:17	I am united with the Lord and one with Him in spirit.
1 Corinthians 6:20	I have been bought with a price; I belong to God.
1 Corinthians 12:27	I am a member of Christ's Body.
Ephesians 1:1	I am a saint.
Ephesians 1:5	I have been adopted as God's child.
Ephesians 2:18	I have direct access to God through the Holy Spirit.
Colossians 1:14	I have been redeemed and forgiven of all my sins.
Colossians 2:10	I am complete in Christ.

I Am Secure in Christ

Romans 8:1-2	I am free from condemnation.
Romans 8:28	I am assured that all things work together for good.
Romans 8:33-34	I am free from any condemning charges against me.
Romans 8:35	I cannot be separated from the love of God.
2 Corinthians 1:21-22	I have been established, anointed and sealed by God.
Philippians 1:6	I am confident that the good work that God has begun in me will be perfected.
Philippians 3:20	I am a citizen of heaven.
Colossians 3:3	I am hidden with Christ in God.
2 Timothy 1:7	I have not been given a spirit of fear but of power, love and a sound mind.
Hebrews 4:16	I can find grace and mercy in time of need.
1 John 5:18	I am born of God and the evil one cannot touch me.

I Am Significant in Christ

Matthew 5:13-14	I am the salt and light of the earth.
John 15:1,5	I am a branch of the true vine, a channel of His life.
John 15:16	I have been chosen and appointed to bear fruit.
Acts 1:8	I am a personal witness of Christ.
1 Corinthians 3:16	I am God's temple.
2 Corinthians 5:17-20	I am a minister of reconciliation.
2 Corinthians 6:1	I am God's coworker.
Ephesians 2:6	I am seated with Christ in the heavenly realm.
Ephesians 2:10	I am God's workmanship.
Ephesians 3:12	I may approach God with freedom and confidence.
Philippians 4:13	I can do all things through Christ who strengthens me.

ANXIETY

Given that every one of us, as believers, is spiritually alive in Christ and our souls are in union with God, why do we still struggle with doubt, fear and anxiety? The answer is twofold. First, in a positive sense, a certain amount of fear is essential for our safety and survival. We should be anxious or concerned for those things we care about. Second, in a negative sense, our minds are programmed to live independently of God. Everything we learned before we asked Christ into our lives is still programmed into our memory bank—there is no delete button—which is why Paul says:

> And do not be conformed to this world, but be transformed by the renewing of your mind, so that you may prove what the will of God is, that which is good and acceptable and perfect (Rom. 12:2).

The primary word for anxiety, *merimna*, in the New Testament has both positive and negative connotations. Of the 25 uses in the New Testament, five indicate a sense of caring, while the other 20 refer to a distracting and negative sense of worry. The root of "merimna" is the verb, *merizo*, which means to draw in different directions or distract. When "merimna" is used as a verb, *merimnao*, it appears to be a conjunction of "merizo" and *nous*, which mean "mind." Perhaps that explains why the *King James Version* of the Bible translated "do not be worried" (Matt. 6:25) as "take no thought," and "why are you worried" (Matt. 6:28) as "why take ye thought."

To be anxious in a negative sense is to be double-minded. We need to recall the passage that teaches that a double-minded person is unstable in all his or her ways (see Jas. 1:8). This also is evident in Matthew 6:24-25:

No one can serve two masters; for either he will hate the one and love the other, or he will be devoted to one and despise the other. You cannot serve God and wealth. For this reason I say to you, do not be worried [anxious] about your life.

The answer according to Jesus is to seek first the kingdom of God and trust our heavenly Father to take care of us.

GOD'S PLAN

Since we are all born dead in our trespasses and sins, we have neither the presence of God in our lives nor the knowledge of His ways. Consequently, we all learn to live our lives independently of God. Let's call this plan B, which is our way by human reason, intuition and experience. Before we invite Jesus Christ into our lives, all we have is plan B.

> WITHOUT GOD WE HAVE NO CHOICE BUT TO TRUST IN OUR OWN LIMITED RESOURCES. WITH GOD WE CAN LIVE SUCCESSFULLY BY TRUSTING IN HIS INFINITE RESOURCES.

Plan A is God's way, which we accept by faith. We learn God's way by choosing to study and believe His Word, which is only made possible by the indwelling presence of God. The apostle

Paul says, "A natural man does not accept the things of the Spirit of God, for they are foolishness to him; and he cannot understand them . . . But we have the mind of Christ" (1 Cor. 2:14,16). The Holy Spirit leads us into all truth (see John 16:13).

God's plan is not just a better way for us to live; it also includes the indwelling presence of God. Without the life of Christ, we cannot live successfully according to the words of Christ. Because our minds have been programmed to live independently of God, we have learned in the past how to cope, succeed and survive without Him; and in the process, we've developed many phobias, insecurities, doubts and uncertainties. Without eternal life, how could we not fear death? Unless we are secure in Christ, how could we not be anxious for tomorrow? We would either have to live in denial or simply not care. Without God we have no choice but to trust in our own limited resources. With God we can live successfully by trusting in His infinite resources.

False Security

Plan B always lurks in the back of our minds. The flesh patterns, strongholds and defense mechanisms will always suggest a way to deal with our life's problems independently of God. This is evident when the struggling Christian asks, "Can I totally trust God, or should I just whisper a prayer and then deal with life as though I am solely responsible for making my own way in this world?" Can we truly say that we trust God if we defend ourselves, meet our own needs and make our own living depending solely on our own resources? Can I cast all my anxieties upon Christ, or do I have to retain some worries in order to make sure everything comes out okay? It is easy to fall back on old ways of coping with life when the pressure is on. Jesus said to the Pharisees, "You are experts at setting aside the commandment of God [plan A] in order to keep your tradition [plan B]" (Mark 7:9).

Such waffling between plan A and plan B creates its own anxieties for carnal Christians. They become double-minded, which brings up an interesting possibility: A natural person could have less anxiety than a carnal Christian who wants the best of both worlds. The natural person only has plan B to deal with and may live relatively anxiety free in his or her own world for a season.

Take the highly educated mathematician who chooses not to believe in God. He creates his own rationalistic worldview and has his own natural explanation of reality. His mind is probably closed to any other explanation. He doesn't like plan A, because it creates a certain amount of anxiety. He works hard to ensure that his family's physical needs and safety are provided for. He doesn't like to think about his purpose for being here or to consider questions about life after death. He has become his own god. Although his plan B may work for a season, the end result is not something he will want: "There is a way which seems right to a man, but its end is the way of death" (Prov. 14:12).

Only a few highly gifted, intelligent, wealthy or naturally strong individuals will find security in their own resources—and then only for a season. Eventually, they too will respond in fear or anxiety when confronted with superior power, intellect or life-threatening circumstances for which they have no answer. Yet for the Christian who is alive in Christ, what power is superior to God and what situation is impossible for Him?

FEAR

Fear is the most basic instinct of every living creature. An animal without fear is likely to become some predator's dinner or just another roadkill. Fear is a natural response when our physical safety or psychological well-being is threatened. Rational fears are learned and vital for our survival. Falling off a chair at an early age develops a healthy respect for heights. Irrational fears, on the other hand, compel us to behave irresponsibly or inhibit us from behaving responsibly. Phobias are irrational fears that reveal developmental problems and/or lack of faith in God.

Fear is different from anxiety, because legitimate fears have an object. In fact, fears or phobias are categorized by their object. The following is a list of some phobias and their object of fear:

- acrophobia—fear of high places
- agoraphobia—fear of open or public places
- claustrophobia—fear of enclosed places
- gephyrophobia—fear of crossing bridges
- hematophobia—fear of blood
- monophobia—fear of being alone
- pathophobia—fear of disease
- toxophobia—fear of being poisoned
- xenophobia—fear of strangers
- zoophobia—fear of animals

In order for a fear object to be legitimate, it must possess two attributes. It must be perceived as imminent (present) and potent (powerful). For example, those who struggle with claustrophobia don't sense any fear until they are actually confronted with the possibility of being in a confined place. Just the thought of such a possibility can cause some to shudder. The womb is an enclosed place, so it is safe to assume that a newborn infant doesn't have claustrophobia. Somehow the fear of confinement was learned, as are most fears. Consequently, they need to be unlearned.

My father-in-law, a United States customs official, saw a small colorful snake on the Arizona border. He fearlessly picked it up and deposited his trophy in a jar. Later he learned it was a coral snake, which appears very harmless, but is one of the most venomous snakes in the Western world. He became flushed with fear when so enlightened. Even though the fear object wasn't imminent, the memory of picking it up made him feel as though it were. Most of us have learned to believe that poisonous snakes are legitimate fear objects. As you read this sentence, you probably sense no fear of snakes, because there are none present (potent but not imminent). However, what if someone threw a rattlesnake into your room and it landed at your feet (imminent and potent)? You probably would be terrorized. Now suppose a dead rattlesnake was thrown at your feet (imminent but not potent). You wouldn't sense any fear provided you were sure it was dead! The fear object is no longer legitimate when just one of its attributes—presence or power—is removed.

The root of most phobias can be traced to the fear of death, the fear of man or the fear of Satan. For example, the fear of dying is the likely root of claustrophobia. Scripture clearly teaches that we don't need to fear any of them, because in each case God has removed one of their attributes. The reality of physical death is always imminent, but the power of death has been broken. Paul teaches that Christ's resurrection rendered physical death no longer potent: "Death is swallowed up in victory. 'O death, where is your victory? O death, where is your sting?'" (1 Cor. 15:54-55). Jesus said, "I am the resurrection and the life; he who believes in Me will live even if he dies, and everyone who lives and believes in Me will never die" (John 11:25-26). In other words, those of us who are born again spiritually will continue to live spiritually even when we die physically. With such a belief, Paul and every born-again believer can say, "For to me, to live is Christ and to die is gain" (Phil. 1:21). We who are free from the fear of death are free to live today.

Many phobias, such as the fear of rejection, the fear of failure, the fear of abandonment and even the fear of death, are rooted in the fear of man. Jesus said, "Do not fear those who kill the body but are unable to kill the soul; but rather fear Him who is able to destroy both soul and body in hell" (Matt. 10:28). Peter said, "Do not fear their intimidation, and do not be troubled, but sanctify Christ as Lord in your hearts, always being ready to make a defense to everyone who asks you to give an account for the hope that is in you, yet with gentleness and reverence" (1 Pet. 3:14-15). The purpose for this verse is obvious if you have ever taught evangelism. The number one reason we as Christians don't share our faith is the fear of man or, more specifically, the fear of rejection.

> THE FEAR OF GOD IS THE ONE FEAR THAT DISPELS ALL OTHER FEARS, BECAUSE HE RULES SUPREME OVER EVERY OTHER FEAR OBJECT INCLUDING SATAN.

Both verses teach us it is God whom we should fear. Two of God's attributes make Him the ultimate fear object in our lives: (1) He is omnipresent (always present), and (2) He is omnipotent (all-powerful). To worship God is to ascribe to Him His divine attributes. We do this for our sakes, which keeps fresh in our minds that our loving heavenly Father is always with us and more powerful than any enemy. The fear of God is the one fear that dispels all other fears, because He rules supreme over every other fear object including Satan. Even though, "Your adversary, the devil, prowls around like a roaring lion, seeking someone to devour" (1 Pet. 5:8), he has been defeated (imminent but not potent). Jesus came for the very purpose of destroying the works of the devil (see 1 John 3:8). "When He had disarmed the rulers and authorities, He made a public display of them, having triumphed over them through Him" (Col. 2:15).

Culturally, we have been programmed to fear everything but God. Scary movies feature King Kong, Godzilla and the Blob, along with the typical parade of psychopathic killers, jealous lovers, criminals and macho men. Then the cultural tide shifted to the occult and alien abductions. In *The Exorcist*, the poor priest was no match for the demonized girl. What a tragic contradiction to Scripture. We have been conditioned to fear men and things that go bump in the night, but we have no fear of God, which is the complete opposite of the fear of the Lord that Scripture teaches. Satan wants to be feared, because he wants to be worshiped.

People and objects are worshiped when their perceived power and value are elevated above ourselves. Only God should have that prominence in our lives, and every child of God is seated with Him in the heavenlies (see Eph. 2:6). We are to worship and fear God, not the defeated god of this world. Fear of any object or personality other than God is mutually exclusive to faith in God. The Bible says, "The fear of the LORD is the beginning of wisdom" (Prov. 9:10). Samuel Johnson said, "Shame rises from the fear of men, conscience rises from the fear of God."[2] Read the ancient wisdom recorded in Isaiah 8:12-13:

You are not to say, "It is a conspiracy!" In regard to all that this people call a conspiracy, and you are not to fear what they fear or be in dread of it. It is the LORD of hosts whom you should regard as holy. And He shall be your fear, and He shall be your dread. Then He shall become a sanctuary.

GOING DEEPER

1. What mental struggles have you had with doubts?
2. To what degree have you struggled with your identity and sense of worth?
3. What is the root meaning of the word "anxiety"?

4. Why do you struggle with plan A (God's plan) versus plan B?

5. How can you grow out of being double-minded?

6. How is fear different from anxiety?

7. What fear objects have you struggled with?

8. Why is God the ultimate fear object?

9. Why do you no longer need to fear death, people and Satan?

10. What happens when you make God your sanctuary?

TAKING EVERY
THOUGHT
CAPTIVE

*Jesus' mission can be described as being twofold: it is a battle against
demons, and it is a battle for men. . . . Anybody who would understand
history must be in possession of the category of the demonic.*

HELMUT THIELICKE

The Bible reveals a continuing struggle between the kingdom of
God and the kingdom of darkness, between the Christ and the
Antichrist, between the Spirit of truth and the father of lies,

between true prophets and false prophets. From the beginning, Satan has opposed God's plan. The serpent planted seeds of doubt in the mind of Eve in the Garden of Eden. She was deceived and Adam sinned (see Gen. 3:1-6).

Adam and Eve were created physically and spiritually alive, but sin resulted in their spiritual death. Consequently, all their descendants are born physically alive but spiritually dead (see Eph. 2:1-10). As newborn infants, we had neither the presence of God in our lives nor the knowledge of His ways, so we all learned to live our lives independently of God. That learned independence is the chief characteristic of the flesh (i.e., old nature), and it is the way our minds have been programmed. In reference to this preconversion mental conditioning and subsequent battle for our minds, Paul writes:

> For though we walk in the flesh, we do not war according to the flesh, for the weapons of our warfare are not of the flesh, but divinely powerful for the destruction of fortresses. We are destroying speculations and every lofty thing raised up against the knowledge of God, and we are taking every thought captive to the obedience of Christ (2 Cor. 10:3-5).

"Fortresses," or "strongholds" in the *King James Version,* are fleshly thought patterns that were programmed into our minds when we learned to live our lives independently of God. Our worldview was shaped by the environment in which we were raised. When we became Christians, nobody pressed the "clear" button. Our old, fleshly, mental, habitual patterns of thought weren't erased.

What was learned has to be unlearned. If we believe a lie, can we renounce that lie and choose to believe the truth? Yes. Repentance literally means a change of mind. Paul teaches that we are transformed by the renewing of our minds (see Rom. 12:2). It is possible to renew our minds because we have the mind of Christ within us, and the Holy Spirit will lead us into all truth. However, the world system in which we were raised and our independent flesh patterns are not the only enemies of our

> TO OVERCOME ALL OUR DOUBTS AND STRANGLEHOLDS OF OUR PASTS, WE HAVE TO REPROGRAM OUR MENTAL COMPUTERS AND CHECK FOR VIRUSES.

sanctification. Even though we are new creations in Christ, we still battle the world, the flesh and the devil. To overcome all our doubts and strangleholds of our pasts, we have to reprogram our mental computers and check for viruses. In this final chapter, I will attempt to explain the spiritual battle for our minds. For a more comprehensive understanding of spiritual warfare, see my book *The Bondage Breaker* (Harvest House Publishers, 2000).

IGNORING SATAN'S DECEPTION

Satan aims to infiltrate our thoughts with his thoughts in order to promote his lies so that we doubt or reject God's truth. Satan knows that if he controls our thoughts, he controls our lives, which is why Paul states in the present tense: "And we are taking every thought captive to the obedience of Christ" (2 Cor. 10:5). In this passage, the word "thought" is the Greek word *noema*. To understand this passage, it is helpful to see how Paul uses this word elsewhere in this second letter to the Corinthian church. "Noema" is only used six times in the Bible, and five of those instances occur in this epistle (see 2:11; 3:14; 4:4; 10:5; 11:3).

After carrying out Church discipline, Paul instructs the Church to forgive:

> But one whom you forgive anything, I forgive also; for indeed what I have forgiven, if I have forgiven anything, I did it for your sakes in the presence of Christ, so that no advantage would be taken of us by Satan, for we are not ignorant of his schemes [noema] (2 Cor. 2:10-11).

Satan does take advantage of those who will not forgive. After helping thousands find their freedom in Christ, I can testify that unforgiveness is the major reason people remain in bondage to the past, and a major reason why Christians struggle with obsessive thoughts.

Paul continues, "And even if our gospel is veiled, it is veiled to those who are perishing, in whose case the god of this world has blinded the minds [noema] of the unbelieving so that they might not see the light of the gospel of the glory of Christ, who is the image of God" (2 Cor. 4:3-4). How are we going to reach this world for Christ if Satan has blinded the minds of unbelievers? Part of the answer is prayer.[1]

Further into the epistle, Paul writes, "But I am afraid that, as the serpent deceived Eve by his craftiness, your minds [noema] will be led astray from the simplicity and purity of devotion to Christ" (2 Cor. 11:3). I am concerned because deception creates doubt and leads to defeat.

Scripture teaches that Satan is capable of putting thoughts into our minds. In the Old Testament, "Satan rose up against Israel and incited David to take a census of Israel" (1 Chron. 21:1, *NIV*). What is wrong with taking a census? Shouldn't David have known how many troops to take into combat? This really reveals the subtle nature of Satan. He knew David had a whole heart for God and would not willingly defy the Lord. Satan's strategy was to convince David to put his confidence in his resources rather than God's resources. Tragically, 70,000 men of Israel fell as the result of David's sin.

How did Satan incite David? Did he audibly talk to David? No, he infiltrated David's thoughts, making David believe Satan's thoughts were his own thoughts. Therein lies the deception. Deceptive thoughts come in such a way that we think they're our own thoughts. I began to realize this years ago while helping others find their freedom in Christ. The battle for the mind is more than mere "self talk." During counseling sessions, I routinely heard people say that they struggle with blasphemous thoughts—all kinds of thoughts raised up against the knowledge of God. These are accusing, questioning and contradicting thoughts like *God doesn't love me. How can I even think I am a Christian? I am no good. Nobody cares about me. Why don't I just end it all?*

Judas also paid attention to a deceiving spirit: "During supper, the devil having already put into the heart of Judas Iscariot, the son of Simon, to betray Him" (John 13:2). We may be tempted to dismiss this as just a bad decision prompted by the flesh, but Scripture clearly says Satan originated those thoughts. When Judas realized what he had done, he took his own life. Jesus warns us: "The thief comes only to steal and kill and destroy" (10:10).

In the Early Church, Satan filled the heart of Ananias to lie to the Holy Spirit (see Acts 5:3). F. F. Bruce, a New Testament scholar, affirms that Ananias was a believer.[2] Ernst Haenchen wrote that Ananias was "a Jewish Christian" and "Satan has filled his heart. Ananias has lied to the Holy Spirit, inasmuch as the Spirit is present in Peter (and in the community). Hence in he last resort it is not simply two men who confront one another, but in them the Holy Spirit and Satan, whose instruments they are."[3]

Martin Luther wrote, "The Devil throws hideous thoughts into the soul—hatred of God, blasphemy and despair." Concerning himself, he said, "When I awake at night, the Devil tarries not to seek me out. He disputes with me and makes me give birth to all kinds of strange thoughts. I think that often the Devil, solely to torment and vex me, wakes me up while I am actually sleeping peacefully. My nighttime combats are much harder for me than in the day. The Devil understands how to produce arguments that exasperate me. Sometimes he has produced such as to make me doubt whether or not there is a God."[4]

Thomas Brooks in his discussion of Satan's devices continually talks of how Satan presents thoughts to the souls of believers.[5] Even David Powlison, who believes that demons cannot invade believers, acknowledges that Satan can put thoughts into one's mind:

> "Voices" in the mind are not uncommon: blasphemous mockeries, spurts of temptation to wallow in vile fantasy or behavior, persuasive lines of unbelief. Classic spiritual warfare interprets these as coming from the evil one.[6]

UNDERSTANDING THE SPIRITUAL BATTLE FOR OUR MINDS

I have counseled hundreds of believers who struggle with their thought life. Some have difficulty concentrating and reading their Bible, while others actually hear "voices" or struggle with accusing and condemning thoughts. With few exceptions, thoughts have proven to be a spiritual battle for their minds. This shouldn't surprise us since we have been forewarned in 1 Timothy 4:1 (*NIV*): "The Spirit clearly says that in later times some will abandon the faith and follow deceiving spirits and things taught by demons."

Why don't believers in Christ know this? One reason is that we really don't have any idea what is going on in the minds of other people unless they have the courage to share with us. In many cases they don't share, because in our culture some people will assume they are mentally ill. Consequently, some may share their negative experiences, but only to the right person would they dare share what is going on inside. Are they mentally ill, or is there a battle being waged for their mind? If we are ignorant of Satan's schemes, we will only come to the conclusion that any problem in the mind must either be a chemical imbalance or a flesh pattern.

Psychologists and psychiatrists routinely see patients who hear voices; a chemical imbalance is the standard diagnosis. Our body chemistry can get out of balance, and hormonal problems can throw our systems off. However, I also believe that other legitimate questions—such as, How can a chemical produce a personal thought? and How can our neurotransmitters involuntarily and randomly fire in such a way that they create thoughts that we are opposed to thinking?—need to be asked. Is there a natural explanation? We must remain open to any legitimate answers and explanations, but I don't think we will have a comprehensive answer unless we take into account the reality of the spiritual world.

How the Brain Works

When people say they hear voices, what do they actually hear? The only way to physically hear with our ears is to have a sound source that compresses air molecules. Sound waves move through the physical medium of air and strike our eardrums, which send a signal to our brains. That is how we physically hear. But voices that people hear or thoughts that they struggle with are not coming from that kind of source if others around them are not also hearing what they hear.

In a similar fashion, when people say they see things that others don't, what are they actually seeing? The only way that we can naturally see something is when a light source reflects off a material object back to our eyes, which sends a signal to our brain. Satan and his demons are spiritual beings; they do not have material substance. Therefore, we cannot see a spiritual being with our natural eyes, nor hear them with our ears:

Think about relationships, crimes, etc...

> For our struggle is not against *flesh and blood*, but against the rulers, against the authorities, against the powers of this dark world and against the spiritual forces of evil in the heavenly realms (Eph. 6:12, emphasis added, *NIV*).

There is a fundamental difference between our brains and our minds. Our brains are organic matter. When we die physically, we separate from our bodies, and our brains eventually return to dust. At the moment of death, we will be absent from our physical bodies and present with the Lord. But we won't be mindless, because the mind is part of the soul.

Our ability to think is similar to how a computer functions. Both have two separate components: (1) the hardware (brain), which is the actual physical computer; and (2) the software (mind), which programs the hardware. If the software is removed from the hardware, it would weigh the same. Likewise, if the Spirit is removed from the body, it also would weigh the same. A computer is totally worthless without the software, but the software won't work either if the hardware shuts down.

Our society assumes that if something is not functioning right between the ears, it must be a hardware problem. I don't believe the primary problem is the hardware; I think the primary problem is the software. If a person has an organic brain syndrome, Down's syndrome or Alzheimer's disease, the brain doesn't function very well. Severe brain damage, however, is relatively rare, and there is little that can be done about it. Romans 12:1-2 says we are to submit our bodies to God, including our brains, and be transformed by the renewing of our minds.

How the Mind Works

We need to understand this spiritual battle for our minds in order to have a comprehensive answer. Let me illustrate why. What typically happens when a frightened child enters his or her parents' bedroom, saying he or she saw or heard something in his or her room? The parents probably go into their child's room, look in the closet or under the bed and say, "There is nothing in your room, honey, now go back to sleep!" However, if you as an adult saw something in your room, would you just forget about it and go back to sleep? "But I looked in the room. There was nothing there," you respond. Because there wasn't anything physical in the room that could be observed by your natural senses, "Then it is not real," says the skeptic. Oh, yes it is! What the child or you saw or heard was in the mind, and it is very real.

> WE DON'T DO ANYTHING WITHOUT FIRST THINKING IT.

I can't explain why people pay attention to deceiving spirits. I don't know how the devil does it, but I don't have to know how he does it in order to believe what Scripture clearly teaches. The spiritual battle for our minds does not operate according to the laws of nature. No physical barriers confine or restrict the movements of Satan. The frightened face of a child testifies that the battle is real.

Much of what is being disgnosed today as mental illness is a manifestation of the battle for our minds. Proverbs 23:7 says, "For as he thinks within himself, so he is." In other words, we don't do anything without first thinking it. All behavior is the product of what we choose to think or believe. We can't see what people think. We can only observe what they do. Trying to change behavior without changing what we think and what we choose to believe will never produce any lasting results.

The need to distinguish between organic mental illness and a spiritual battle for our minds is illustrated in this testimony I received by e-mail:

> I wanted to thank you for showing me how to be free of something I always suspected was spiritual but was never quite sure. For years, ever since I was a teenager (I am now 36), I had these "voices" in my head. There were four in particular and sometimes what seemed like loud choruses of them. When the subject of schizophrenia would come up on television or in a magazine, I would think to myself, *I know I am not schizophrenic, but what is this in my head?*
>
> I was tortured, mocked and jeered; every single thought I had was second-guessed. Consequently, I had zero self-esteem. I often wished the voices would be quiet, and I always wondered if other people heard voices as well—and if it was "common."
>
> When I started to learn from you about taking every thought captive to the obedience of Christ and read about other people's experiences with these voices, I came to recognize them for what they were, and I was able to make them leave.
>
> This was an amazing and beautiful thing: to be fully quiet in my mind, after so many years of torment. I do

not need to explain further all the wonderful things that come with this freedom of the mind; it is a blessing you seem to know well.

Paul admonishes us to put on the armor of God (see Eph. 6:10-18). The belt of truth defends us against the father of lies. The breastplate of righteousness protects us against the accuser of the brethren. Paul summarizes by saying, "In addition to all, taking up the shield of faith with which you will be able to extinguish all the flaming arrows of the evil one" (v. 16). The "flaming arrows," or "fiery darts" in the *New King James Version*, are just tempting, accusing and deceptive thoughts that every one of us has to deal with. Those of us who are healthy Christians don't pay attention to them because we know the truth and choose to believe it. Yet what happens if we don't take every thought captive to the obedience of Christ? If we entertain such thoughts, we will be deceived and doubts will creep into our minds.

Where Thoughts Come From

How do we know whether negative, lying and condemning thoughts are from the evil one or from our own flesh patterns? Don't assume that all obsessive thoughts come from Satan. Whether the thought in your mind came from the television set, your memory bank, from the pit or from your own imagination, it doesn't make any difference in one sense, because the answer is the same. We are to take *every* thought captive to the obedience of Christ. We must choose to think and believe the truth. If it isn't true, don't believe it. Thoughts do not originate in us if they are gone after we submit to God and resist the devil in genuine repentance. Flesh patterns don't leave—they are slowly replaced or overcome as we renew our minds. Paul says we are not to be anxious (double-minded) about anything. Rather we are to turn to God in prayer, "And the peace of God, which surpasses all comprehension, will guard your hearts and your minds [noema] in Christ Jesus" (Phil. 4:7). The next verse instructs us to let our minds dwell on those things that are true, pure, lovely and right.

We could try to analyze where every thought came from, but that wouldn't resolve the dilemma of our thoughts. We only would get caught up in our own subjective maze. Too much time is spent in the paralysis of analysis. Providing a brilliant analysis of why we have obsessive thoughts doesn't solve the problem.

Mental strongholds can be torn down, not by analyzing, but by reprogramming our minds. If we learned to do something the wrong way, we can learn to do it the right way. If we have believed a lie, we can decide to renounce the lie and choose to believe the truth. However, it will take the rest of our lives to renew our minds and mature in Christ. Our minds will never be fully renewed, and our character will always fall short of perfection, but that is our pursuit. The growth process will be stopped, however, if we do not resolve our personal and spiritual conflicts through genuine repentance and faith in God. Those living in bondage go from book to book, program to program, pastor to pastor, counselor to counselor; but nothing seems to work. They don't grow, because they are chained to the past. They have unresolved issues between themselves and God, which keep them from experiencing His grace. They are distracted and deceived by the father of lies.

WINNING THE BATTLE

Think of your mind as a coffee pot. You desire the water inside to be pure, but unfortunately, you have added coffee grounds. There is no way to filter out the coffee once it has been added, so the water inside becomes dark and polluted. Sitting beside the coffee pot is a huge bowl of crystal-clear ice, which represents the

Word of God. You can only put in one or two cubes a day, so your efforts at clearing up the dark, polluted water seem futile at first. But over the course of time, the water begins to look less polluted. When you taste the water to which you once added coffee grounds, you can hardly taste or smell the presence of the coffee anymore. The process works provided you stop putting in more coffee grounds.

For most of us this process of winning the battle for our minds will initially take two steps forward and one step back. With persistence it becomes three steps forward and one step back, and then four and five steps forward and one step back, as we learn to take every thought captive in obedience to Christ. We may despair with all the backward steps, but God will not give up on us. Remember, our sins are already forgiven. We only need to keep living by faith and taking every thought captive in obedience to Christ, which means we don't need to think about anything but the truth.

This war *is* winnable since we are already alive in Christ and dead to sin. Christ already won the bigger battle. Freedom to be all God calls us to be is the greatest blessing in this present life. This freedom is worth fighting for. As we learn more about who we are as children of God and the nature of the battle that is being waged in our minds, the process gets easier. Eventually it will be 20 steps forward and 1 step back, and then finally, the steps will all move forward with only an occasional slip in the battle for our minds.

Paul writes, "Let the peace of Christ rule in your hearts, since as members of one body you were called to peace. And be thankful" (Col. 3:15, *NIV*). How we let the peace of Christ rule in our hearts is explained in the next verse: "Let the word of Christ dwell in you richly" (v. 16, *NIV*). We must fill our minds with the crystal-clear Word of God; there is no alternative plan. Just trying to stop thinking bad thoughts will not work. Rebuking obsessive thoughts also will not work. We are only treading water, and we will make no progress in overcoming our doubts. We will be like a person in the middle of a lake who tries to keep 12 corks submerged with a small hammer while treading water. If this describes you, what should you do? Ignore the stupid corks and swim to shore! We are not called to dispel the darkness; we are called to turn on the light. We overcome the father of lies by choosing the truth.

> YOU CAN'T EXPECT GOD TO BLESS YOU IF YOU ARE LIVING IN OPEN REBELLION TO HIM.

The psalmist wrote, "How can a young man keep his way pure? By living according to your word. I seek you with all my heart; do not let me stray from your commands. I have hidden your word in my heart that I might not sin against you" (Ps. 119:9-11, *NIV*). There is a peace of God, which surpasses all comprehension, which will guard your hearts and your minds (noema) in Christ Jesus (see Phil. 4:7).

Finally, brethren, whatever is true, whatever is honorable, whatever is right, whatever is pure, whatever is lovely, whatever is of good repute, if there is any excellence and if anything worthy of praise, dwell on these things. The things you have learned and received and heard and seen in me, practice these things, and the God of peace will be with you (Phil. 4:8-9).

You can ignore the corks and swim to shore if you are experiencing your freedom in Christ. If you have a lot of unresolved conflicts, however, you are just treading water. Your relationship with God is personal, and like any relationship, certain issues need to be resolved in order for the relationship to work. You can't expect God to bless you if you are living in open rebellion to Him. "Rebellion is like the sin of divination, and arrogance like the evil of idolatry" (1 Sam. 15:23, *NIV*). If you are proud, God is opposed to you (see Jas. 4:6). If you are bitter and unwilling to forgive, God will turn you over to the torturers (see Matt. 18:34). These issues have to be resolved first since only God can bind up the brokenhearted and set the captives free.

GOING DEEPER

1. How are strongholds formed in your mind?
2. In the process of reprogramming your mind, why do you have to check for "viruses"?
3. In 2 Corinthians, explain the connection between noema (mind or thoughts) and spiritual warfare.
4. Why is it important to know that some of your thoughts may not be your own? What kind of wrong conclusions can you draw if you don't understand this?
5. Why does the secular world come to conclusions about mental illness that differ from those of informed Christians?
6. Why must you take every thought captive to the obedience of Christ? How do you do that?
7. How can you reprogram your mind?
8. Should you argue with or try to rebuke all negative thoughts? Why or why not?

9. What happens if you just try not to think negative thoughts but haven't truly repented (i.e., you haven't resolved issues between yourself and God that are critical)?

10. Would you be willing to read *The Steps to Freedom in Christ* and work through the Steps?

E P I L O G U E

For 15 years, Freedom in Christ Ministries has been helping people all over the world resolve their personal and spiritual conflicts through genuine repentance and faith in God. The discipleship tool we use is *The Steps to Freedom in Christ*—or Steps. The Steps can be purchased from our office or from any Christian bookstore. Many Christians can work through the process on their own. However, some cannot and need the help of a godly pastor or counselor. To know how to minister these Steps, read *Discipleship Counseling* (Regal Books, 2003).

Helping Christians find their freedom in Christ requires a wholistic answer, which takes into account the reality of the spiritual world. It also requires an understanding and intentional inclusion of Christ and the Holy Spirit in the process. God is the wonderful counselor and the great physician. Only He can bind up the brokenhearted and set the captives free. He is the

One who grants "repentance leading to the knowledge of the truth" (2 Tim. 2:25).

Research has been conducted on the Steps discipleship counseling process in several churches in conjunction with our Living Free in Christ conference. The participants included those who requested further assistance after hearing the message. They were given one extended counseling session with a trained encourager. They took a pretest before the conference, and then a posttest three months later. The following are the results of this research:

Depression	57 percent improvement
Anxiety	54 percent improvement
Fear	49 percent improvement
Anger	55 percent improvement
Tormenting thoughts	50 percent improvement
Negative habits	53 percent improvement
Self-image	56 percent improvement

The reason this process is so effective is *not* because I or anyone else is a wonderful counselor. Actually, trained lay encouragers did all the counseling for the purpose of this research. It is effective because the Lord is the One who sets them free. Christians bond with their loving heavenly Father after they resolve their personal and spiritual conflicts, and the Holy Spirit bears witness with their spirit that they are children of God. You, too, can find your freedom in Christ through genuine repentance and faith in God. When you do, your Bible will come alive, and you will grow in the grace and knowledge of our Lord and Savior Jesus Christ. May the good Lord grant you that repentance.

For additional information on resources and conferences contact:

FREEDOM IN CHRIST MINISTRIES

9051 Executive Park Drive, Suite 503
Knoxville, Tennessee 37923
Phone: (865) 342-4000
Fax: (865) 342-4001
E-Mail: info@ficm.org
Website: http://www.ficm.org

ENDNOTES

Chapter One

1. Dale Carnegie, quoted in Sherwood Eliot et al., *Living Quotations for Christians* (New York: Harper and Row, 1974), p. 65.
2. Source unknown.
3. Neil T. Anderson, *Victory over the Darkness*, 2nd ed. (Ventura, CA: Regal Books, 2000), pp. 115-117.

Chapter Two

1. Adrian Plass, *The Sacred Diary of Adrian Plass* (London: Marshal Morgan and Scott Publications, 1987) pp. 19-23.
2. Dwight L. Moody, quoted in Sherwood Eliot et al., *Living Quotations for Christians* (New York: Harper and Row, 1974), p. 76.
3. For more information on the spiritual dynamics of prayer, see Neil Anderson, *Praying by the Power of the Spirit* (Eugene, OR: Harvest House Publishers, 2003).
4. Dr. and Mrs. Howard Taylor, *Hudson Taylor's Spiritual Secret* (Chicago: Moody Press, 1990), pp. 158-164.

Chapter Three

1. Victor Frankl, quoted in George Sweeting, *Great Quotes and Illustrations* (Waco, TX: Word Books, 1985), p. 143.
2. Martin Luther, quoted in Frank Mead, *The Encyclopedia of Religious Quotations* (Westwood, NJ: Fleming H. Revell, 1965), p. 234.

Chapter Four

1. Neil T. Anderson and Hal Baumchen, *Finding Hope Again* (Ventura, CA: Regal Books, 1999), pp. 198-200.

Chapter Five

1. Jim Elliot, *The Journals of Jim Elliot* (Grand Rapids, MI: Fleming H. Revell, 1978) p. 174.
2. Bob Moorehead, *Words Aptly Spoken* (n.p.: Overlake Christian Bookstore, 1995).

Chapter Six

1. Lucinda Bassett, *Overcoming Your Anxiety and Fear.* Midwest Center for Stress and Anxiety, Inc., videocassette.
2. Samuel Johnson, quoted in George Sweeting, *Great Quotes and Illustrations* (Waco, TX: Word Books, 1985), p. 115.

Chapter Seven

1. Neil Anderson, *Praying by the Power of the Spirit* (Eugene, OR: Harvest House Publishers, 2003).
2. F. F. Bruce, *Commentary on the Book of Acts* (Grand Rapids, MI: Eerdmans Publishing, 1954), p. 114.
3. Ernst Haenchen, *The Acts of the Apostles* (Philadelphia: Westminster Press, 1971), p. 237.
4. Martin Luther, *Table Talk,* vol. 4 (New Canaan, CT: Keats Publishing, 1979), quoted in Father Louis Coulange [Joseph Turmel], *The Life of the Devil* (London: Alfred A. Knopf, 1929), pp. 147-148.
5. Thomas Brooks, *Precious Remedies Against Satan's Devices* (London: The Banner of Truth Trust, 1968), n.p.
6. David Powlison, *Power Encounters: Reclaiming Spiritual Warfare* (Grand Rapids, MI: Baker Book House, 1995), p. 135.

Books and Resources by
Dr. Neil T. Anderson

Core Message and Materials

The Bondage Breaker and study guide and audiobook (Harvest House Publishers, 2000)—with well over 1 million copies in print, this book explains spiritual warfare, what our protection is, ways that we are vulnerable and how we can live a liberated life in Christ.

Breaking Through to Spiritual Maturity (Regal Books, 2000)—this curriculum teaches the basic message of Freedom in Christ Ministries.

Discipleship Counseling and videocassettes (Regal Books, 2003)—combines the concepts of discipleship and counseling, and the practical integration of theology and psychology, for helping Christians resolve their personal and spiritual conflicts through repentance.

The Steps to Freedom in Christ and interactive videocassette (Regal Books, 2000)—this discipleship counseling tool helps Christians resolve their personal and spiritual conflicts.

Victory over the Darkness and study guide, audiobook and video-cassettes (Regal Books, 2000)—with well over 1 million copies in print, this core book explains who you are in Christ, how you walk by faith, how your mind and emotions function and how to relate to one another in Christ.

Specialized Books

The Biblical Guide to Alternative Medicine with Dr. Michael Jacobson (Regal Books, 2003)—develops a grid by which you can evaluate medical practices. It applies the grid to the world's most recognized philosophies of medicine and health.

Blessed Are the Peacemakers with Dr. Charles Mylander (Regal Books, 2002)—explains the ministry of reconciliation and gives practical steps for being reconciled with others.

Breaking the Bondage of Legalism with Rich Miller and Paul Travis (Harvest House Publishers, 2003)—an exposure and explanation of legalism and how to overcome it.

The Christ-Centered Marriage with Dr. Charles Mylander (Regal Books, 1997)—explains God's divine plan for marriage and the steps that couples can take to resolve their difficulties.

Christ-Centered Therapy with Dr. Terry and Julianne Zuehlke (Zondervan Publishing House, 2000)—a textbook explaining the practical integration of theology and psychology for professional counselors.

Daily in Christ with Joanne Anderson (Harvest House Publishers, 2000)—this popular daily devotional is being used by thousands of Internet subscribers every day.

Finding Hope Again with Hal Baumchen (Regal Books, 1999)—explains depression and how to overcome it.

Freedom from Addiction with Mike and Julia Quarles (Regal Books, 1997)—using Mike's testimony, this book explains the nature of chemical addictions and how to overcome them in Christ.

Freedom from Fear with Rich Miller (Harvest House Publishers, 1999)—explains fear, anxiety and disorders, and how to overcome them.

Freedom in Christ Bible (Zondervan Publishing House, 2002)—a one-year discipleship study with notes in the Bible.

Getting Anger Under Control with Rich Miller (Harvest House Publishers, 1999)—explains the basis for anger and how to control it.

God's Power at Work in You with Dr. Robert L. Saucy (Harvest House Publishers, 2001)—a thorough analysis of sanctification and practical instruction on how we grow in Christ.

Leading Teens to Freedom in Christ with Rich Miller (Regal Books, 1997)—this discipleship counseling book focuses on teenagers, their problems and how to solve them.

One Day at a Time with Mike and Julia Quarles (Regal Books, 2000)—this devotional helps those who struggle with addictive behaviors and how to discover the grace of God on a daily basis.

Released from Bondage with Dr. Fernando Garzon and Judith E. King (Thomas Nelson, 2002)—contains personal accounts of bondage with explanatory notes showing how people found their freedom in Christ, and how the message of Freedom in Christ can be applied to therapy with research results.

The Seduction of Our Children with Steve Russo (Harvest House Publishers, 1991)—explains what teenagers are experiencing and how parents can be equipped to help them.

Setting Your Church Free with Dr. Charles Mylander (Regal Books, 1994)—this book on Christian leadership also explains corporate bondage and how it can be resolved in Christ.

The Spiritual Protection of Our Children with Peter and Sue Vander Hook (Regal Books, 1996)—using the Vander Hook's experience, this book explains how parents can help their children.

A Way of Escape with Russ Rummer (Harvest House Publishers, 1998)—explains sexual strongholds and how they can be torn down in Christ.

Who I Am in Christ (Regal Books, 2001)—describes in 36 short chapters who you are in Christ and how He meets your deepest needs.

VICTORY OVER THE DARKNESS SERIES

Overcoming Negative Self-Image with Dave Park (Regal Books, 2003)
Overcoming Addictive Behavior with Mike Quarles (Regal Books, 2003)
Overcoming Depression with Joanne Anderson (Regal Books, 2004)
Overcoming Doubt (Regal Books, 2004)

THE BONDAGE BREAKER SERIES

Finding Freedom in a Sex-Obsessed World (Harvest House Publishers, 2004)

Finding God's Will in Spiritually Deceptive Times (Harvest House Pub-lishers, 2003)

Praying by the Power of the Spirit (Harvest House Publishers, 2003)

YOUTH BOOKS

Awesome God with Rich Miller (Harvest House Publishers, 1996)

The Bondage Breaker—Youth Edition with Dave Park (Harvest House Publishers, 2001)

Extreme Faith with Dave Park (Harvest House Publishers, 1996)

Higher Ground with Dave Park and Dr. Robert L. Saucy (1999)*

Purity Under Pressure with Dave Park (Harvest House Publishers, 1995)

Radical Image with Dave Park and Dr. Robert L. Saucy (Harvest House Publishers, 1998)*

Real Life with Dave Park (Harvest House Publishers, 2000)*

Reality Check with Rich Miller (Harvest House Publishers, 1996)

Righteous Pursuit with Dave Park (Harvest House Publishers, 2000)

Stomping Out Depression with Dave Park (Regal Books, 2001)

Stomping Out Fear with Rich Miller and Dave Park (Harvest House Publishers, 2003)

Stomping Out the Darkness with Dave Park (Regal Books, 1999)

Ultimate Love with Dave Park (Harvest House Publishers, 1996)

* Available from Freedom in Christ Ministries only